ONE CIVIL SERVANT'S
WORLD WAR II

1939 TO 1945

BY HARRY WILLIAM SEMARK

*This book is dedicated with love
to Joyce, my wife for
64 years beginning in 1939.*

ONE CIVIL SERVANT'S
WORLD WAR II

1939 TO 1945

BY HARRY WILLIAM SEMARK

Published by Memoirs

MEMOIRS
PUBLISHING

25 Market Place, Cirencester, Gloucestershire, GL7 2NX
info@memoirsbooks.co.uk www.memoirspublishing.com

Copyright ©Harry William Semark, November 2012
First published in England, November 2012

ISBN 978-1-909304-83-3

Printed in England

CONTENTS

LIST OF APPENDICES

ACKNOWLEDGEMENTS

I should like to thank the following persons and organisations for their generous assistance in supplying photographs and information and typing in relation to the book:

Mrs Mandy George, for typing the book ready for publication.

H A Richards, City Librarian, Archives Information Service, Southampton City Council, City Gate, Southampton.

Jean Lear and Susan Fowler, Local Study Librarians, Medway Archives and Local Studies Centre, Civic Centre, Strood, Rochester, Kent.

Mrs Sue Millican, Great Yarmouth Library, Tolhouse Street, Great Yarmouth, Norfolk.

Mrs Adel Butler, Librarian, The Corporation of Trinity House, Tower Hill, London.

Mr R Thomas, Curator, Holman Museum, Camborne, Cornwall.

Mr Harold Bennett, Chatham Dockyard Historical Society, The Museum Chatham Historical Dockyard, Chatham, Kent.

Keith Birlwhistle, Research Assistant, The Royal Navy Submarine Museum, Haslar Jetty Road, Gosport, Hants.

Phillip Rood, Vosper Thornycroft (UK) Ltd, Victoria Road, Woolston, Southampton.

Mrs Lois Pratt, Sheerness Library, Russel Street, Sheerness, Kent

Liza Verity, Information Specialist and Helen Pethers, Senior Library

Assistant, National Maritime Museum, Greenwich, London.

Miss Alison Frazer MA, Principal Archivist, Loing Street Library, Kirkwall, Orkney.

Miss Pamela Clark, Registrar, The Royal Archives, The Royal Collection Trust, Windsor Castle, Berks.

Peter Donnerly, Lieutenant Commander, Royal New Zealand Navy, Director of the Royal New Zealand Navy Museum, Devonport, Auckland.

Mr S Courtney, Curator Royal Naval Museum, HM Naval Base, Portsmouth, Hampshire.

Mrs Lin Vine, Curator, Queenborough Guildhall Museum, Queenborough, Kent.

Mr Marc Farrance, Visitors Services Officer, "Explosion Museum of Naval Fire Power" Priddy's Hard, Gosport, Hampshire.

Mr Joe Carr, Curator, Great Yarmouth Museums, Norfolk Museums and Archaeology Service.

Penny Rudkin, City Library Archives and Information Services, Southampton City Council, Civic Centre, Southampton.

David Taylor, Picture Library National Museum, London.

Mr Brad King MA, Director of HMS Belfast, Morgan's Lane, Tooley Street, London, SE1 2JH.

Nick Hewitt, Interpretation Officer, HMS Belfast, London.

LIST OF ILLUSTRATIONS

FOREWORD

**By Commodore Rob Thompson BSc MA CEng
FIMarEST
Naval Base Commander, Portsmouth**

Perhaps one of the most memorable sights in the Second World War was the arrival in Scapa Flow of the Home Fleet after the successful sinking of Scharnhörst in the last week of 1943. Harry Semark was one of the few civilians privileged to witness it. This and other of his eye witness accounts, remembered with such clarity down the years, add value to the record of what was a monumentous six years in the history of not only these isles but most of the world.

This book describes with complete accuracy and in a most unassuming way, the real story of the varied service that one man, like thousands of others, gave ungrudgingly largely unnoticed and unrewarded, to keep the Naval War machine, ready to fight and win.

Short notice moves and long separations were accepted stoically and small pleasures taken where and when they could be. Throughout the whole narrative there is a never wavering sense of worth, of behaving appropriately, of duty and self-sacrifice.

Harry Semark makes light of the hardships the world often worked in, in biting weather on large guns with practically no assistance, being expected to analyse and make good faults as requested by the Gunnery Officer (this was World War II practice). It is to his credit that he invariably found a way to achieve the aim, be it converting a fishing drifter for its self protection to modifying a battleship's 15" guns to allow it to engage and destroy the enemy.

A technical expert, he makes gunfitting come alive, this obvious zest for knowledge and life ensures that the cameos he paints are always vital and fascinating.

It is a great pleasure to me to be allowed this opportunity of drawing attention to the story of a very expert and able man's activities in support of the country.

CHAPTER 1

The Year 1939

H.M. Gunwharf Chatham and H.M. Dockyard Chatham

Virtually everyone that experienced World War II, 1939 to 1945, had a story to tell, that reflected the wide ranging activities of those hazardous and eventful years.

This is one such true story, of how while serving as a civilian, Civil Service gun fitter, with the Royal Naval Armament Supply Department of the Admiralty, I spent the War years examining, repairing and modifying the guns and anti-submarine weapons of the Royal Navy, the Navies of Australia and New Zealand and the ships of the allies.

It all started on the 21st February 1939, when at the age of 25, I passed the fitter's trade test at H.M. Gunwharf Chatham, Kent (F.1 refers). Situated on the right bank of the R Medway, in close proximity to the town of Chatham, the Gunwharf was one of many Armament Depots distributed at that time throughout the United Kingdom and the British Empire. The Gunwharf had a long association with both military and naval armaments dating back to 1666 (App 2 refers).

So having passed the trade test, and signed an Official Secrets Act form, I commenced work in the Depot's gun repair workshop, little thinking that I would serve 39 years from 1939 to1978 with the Department, serving at various Depots and Naval Bases, including a 6 month spell of duty during 1943 at Scapa Flow in the Orkneys servicing the guns of the Home Fleet.

Fortunately, a number of my activities prior to 1939, combined to prove a great asset in my new job. These activities included attending Rochester Technical College from the age of 11 to 15 years, where both theoretical and practical engineering were high on the agenda. This was followed by a four year apprenticeship as a fitter at Messrs Aveling and Porters, steam engineers of Strood in Kent, while from 1931 to 1935 starting at the age of 18, I served in the Territorial Army with "Rochester's Own" Battery of the Royal Artillery, manning 9.2" and 6" coast defence guns and smaller calibre anti aircraft guns and this training gave me a sound knowledge

F.1 - H.M. Gunwharf Chatham, an Armament Depot from
1666 to 1958 (Official Photo)

F.2 - Keeping fit in 1939; the author does a headstand, in sight of the R Medway in Kent

of guns and their breech mechanisms.

Also, running parallel with these activities, I pursued my hobbies of physical training (F.2) and wrestling and appeared in a number of professional 11 stone, middle weight contests in the London and Gillingham, Kent, areas, although I never had any intention of making a career of wrestling. Both these hobbies stood me in good stead on several occasions during the War.

Working conditions in the gun repair workshop and the general atmosphere among staff and officials was excellent, and I soon settled down to enjoy the work, which was of a very exacting nature. For the first two months or so, my efforts were directed to repairing the components of 4" calibre Breech Loading (BL) guns, of World War I (1914 to 1918) vintage. Guns of this type were installed on Defensively Equipped Merchant ships and ships of the Fleet Auxiliary Service.

This was followed by work on 3" and 4" calibre, Quick Firing (QF) guns which were suitable for both surface firing and anti aircraft use.

In relation to Breech Loading (BL) guns, they were introduced into the Royal Navy around the 1860's and over the years were redesigned and modified to become the BL guns of World War II (F.3).

The Quick Firing gun was introduced into naval service in 1884, as a defence against fast moving torpedo boats. The 6 Pdr (1884) and the 3 Pdr (1886) Hotchkiss QF guns were among the first to be accepted into service. With the advent of air warfare in World War I, some of these early QF guns were utilized for anti-aircraft purposes. F.4 shows anti-aircraft guns of World War II. Further information on Breech Loading and Quick Firing guns is given in App 5.

F.3 The Breech of a 6" Mk XXIII BL Gun, open ready for loading
(Official Photo)

Then around late May 1939, as gun work aboard ships of the Fleet began to build up, I was delighted to be detailed to join the Depot's Afloat Party, working on guns aboard Royal Navy vessels in the adjoining H.M.S. Dockyard Chatham (App 3).

This was an outstanding opportunity to greatly improve one's knowledge of guns and their associated machinery, aboard ships of various types and included working in gun turrets and attending gun trials at sea.

F.4 - Loading a set of twin 4" Mk XVI Quick Firing guns
(Official Photo)

The Afloat Party consisted of six or seven gun fitters, each fitter having a "fitter's mate" to assist with lifting, cleaning and greasing gun parts. Two more men made up the Afloat Party, and their function was to clean out the bores of the guns, ready for inspection and measuring purposes, and to re-grease them when this was completed. They also took gutta-percha impression of suspect sections of the rifling of guns, also for inspection purposes.

A Chargeman of fitters, based in a small wooden hut in the

Dockyard was responsible for the Afloat Party, and visited his far flung "flock", mounted on a red bicycle, supplied by the Admiralty.

The final inspection of guns, depth charge throwers etc. was carried out by members of the Naval Ordnance Inspectorate, a department founded on 1st April 1908, with the creation of the post of Chief Inspector of Naval Ordnance at the Admiralty. From then on it grew into a large department, dedicated to the safe use of naval armaments.

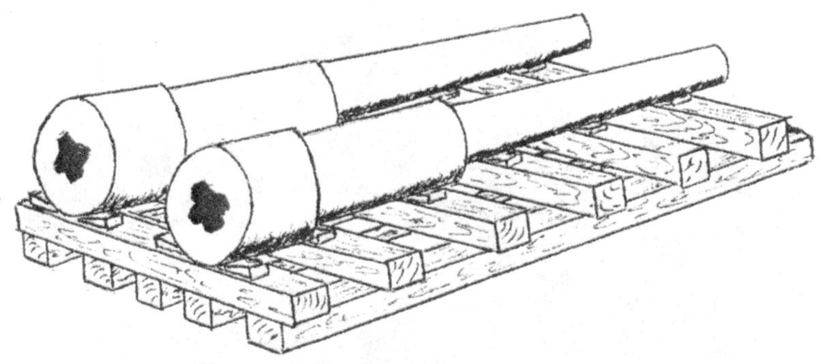

F.5 - 15" Gun barrels stored in the open, on huge baulks of timber on the Gun Ground, in Chatham Dockyard

Also situated in the dockyard was a special open space, known as the Gun Ground, where as many as forty gun barrels were preserved, and stored, in the open on huge baulks of timber (F.5). The guns ranged in calibres from 3" to the mighty 15" guns fitted to battleships, battle-cruisers, and monitors.

In order to lift these guns, including the 15" guns, which weighed 97 tons 3 cwt (98.729 tonnes), a massive 100 ton gantry crane straddled the Gun Ground and ran on rails the 50 yards or so length of the Gun Ground.

A small bungalow type of brick building situated on the

Gun Ground provided the "headquarters" of the Afloat Party, and from there they worked on ships' guns throughout the Dockyard.

I worked many times on the Gun Ground, often fitting and adjusting breech mechanisms to guns different from those to which they were originally fitted, a process known as "mating a breech mechanism to a gun".

During one particular period on the Gun Ground, I "mated" five 8" Mk VIII BL guns, of the same type as those used by H.M.S. Exeter at the Battle of the River Plate on 13th December 1939. Each of these guns weighed 16 tons 16½ cwt (approx. 16,825kg) and the breech mechanism weighed 7½ cwt (375 kg). On completion of this work each gun was "passed out" by a Naval Ordnance Examiner, with me standing by to assist as required.

F.6 - The 8,250 ton cruiser H.M.S. York
(Photo: Royal Naval Museum, H.M. Naval Base, Portsmouth)

I also carried out work on a series of destroyers, several of which were in dry dock, receiving attention to their hulls, propellers, etc. Many of these destroyers were of the "V" and

"W" Class, built during 1917-1919, with such names as "Verdun", "Veteran", "Wanderer" and "Wolfhound".

Work on these guns went well, although extra care was always required for safety reasons when working on ships in dry dock, especially in wet weather, when the ships steel decks got very slippery.

Shortly after this I got my first "big ship", the 8,250 ton cruiser H.M.S. York, sister ship to H.M.S. Exeter. H.M.S. York (F.6) was an elegant looking ship, with a complement of 600 men, and was built at Palmer's Shipyard on the Tyne from 1928 to 1930. Her main armament consisted of six 8" Mk VIII BL guns, housed in three gun turrets, with two guns, one right hand and one left hand in each turret.

The 8" gun turret was the gun fitter's nightmare, owing to the cramped working conditions, and both the fitter and his "mate" received 1s 6d extra per day, while employed in 8" BL gun turrets; this was known as "confined space allowance".

To reach the gun area of the turret, one had to stoop almost double, between the deck of the ship and the underside of the turret and enter through a heavy steel trap door, held open by means of a spring loaded steel catch. This manoeuvre left very little room for error and one of our fitters had been severely injured when one of the steel trap doors crashed down on to his foot, an episode that made the whole of the Afloat Party extremely wary of turret trap doors.

Once inside the turret, the fitter worked on the breech mechanism while standing on a narrow steel grid platform, suspended over a 20 feet (6.1m) or so deep "gun well", into which the breech end of the gun descended when the gun was elevated. It was indeed a well earned, but never the less very welcome 1s 6d.

My first action on going aboard the "York", as aboard all the ships I worked on, was to contact the Chief Ordnance Artificer, and inform him that I had arrived to carry out the work as required by the Gunnery Officer and at the same time to obtain permission to use the ship's Ordnance Workshop if required.

The specific task on this occasion was to fit a new gear box to one of the 8" guns and to carry out a routine examination and adjustment as required to its breech mechanism.

The gear box, with its thick bronze casing, weighed in the region of 112lbs (approx 50 kg) and when "clutched in", enabled the breech to be opened and closed manually, by means of a bronze hand wheel. The gear box fitted onto a "shoulder" projecting from the side of the gun. After being "bedded down" on the "shoulder" it was secured in position by a number of large screws.

With the help of my "fitter's mate" to manipulate the lifting gear attached to the roof of the turret by an eye bolt, the gear box took the best part of two days to fit and finally assemble.

After the remainder of the work on the breech mechanism had been completed, the work passed its examinations, during which the 7½ cwt (375kg) breech mechanism operated smoothly through the open and closed positions.

There were however two incidences of a lighter nature during my stay on the "York". One occurred while I was stretching my legs on the upper deck, when a cry of "there she goes" sent a group of us scrambling up the "York's" super-structure in an attempt to catch sight of the cruiser H.M.S. Euryalus being launched in a distant part of the Dockyard. It was the 6th June 1939.

The other incident centred around a jovial sporty member of the gun's crew known as "Tubby", a stocky, powerfully built man, who had represented the Royal Navy in the Royal Tournament, at its London venue.

He also possessed a thick rubber "chest expander" that was his constant companion, and he good humorously offered to give it to any "Dockyard Matey" who could stretch it to arms' length. However despite having achieved County Standards on the Front and Overhead pulls with spring steel chest expanders during my training for wrestling, I gently resisted his constant requests to "come on, have a go", so he ceased to pursue the matter, which I mentally put to rest.

But fate decided otherwise, when one morning right out of the blue, up pops "Tiny" Ridd, a middle aged gentle giant, employed as a Gun Mounting fitter in the Dockyard, and at that time working on the machinery that operated the gun turret. "Tiny" was a close friend and wrestling fan of mine, who I met on a regular basis as we moved around from ship to ship. On this occasion he was beaming all over this face, as he informed me that he had accepted a friendly challenge on my behalf with a fellow named "Tubby" who had a rubber "chest expander". Surely this was where we came in.

So during the lunch break, unable to resist any longer, I made my way, accompanied by "Tiny" as my "second" to the appointed rendezvous below deck. "Tubby" was already there, looking more jovial than ever, having at least found someone to "have a go". He was surrounded by a group of Dockyard men, who had already fixed the odds at 50 to 1 in favour of the rubber expander.

"Tubby" acting as the adjudicator, laid down the rule that it should be a Front Pull, which pleased me very much for although one of the most difficult, it was never the less one of my best. He also reaffirmed his offer that whoever pulled the expander could keep it.

This I declined to accept and explained that should I succeed, I would not under any circumstances deprive him of the expander that so obviously gave him so much pleasure. To this, ever a good sport, he finally, but reluctantly agreed and amid a general murmur of approval from the Dockyard men, all was ready to start.

So taking a firm grip on the two ball-shaped ends of the expander, and holding it at arms' length and at shoulder height in front of me, I took a preliminary pull. The expander was as solid as a rock, not a good sign, but I continued with a steady pull, thankful for all those years of physical training, and then felt what I wanted, an almost imperceptible movement in the expander, signalling that its inertia was being overcome. Then, mustering a final effort, I applied a sustained pull that stretched the expander to the limit required of the pull, and then, while still retaining full control of the expander, allowed it to return to its starting position and repeated the pull a second time, much to my own pleasure, and after shaking hands with "Tubby", handed him back his prized possession and wished him all the best for the future.

"Tiny" my friend and "publicity agent", was still busy telling all within earshot, "I told you so", while the Dockyard men gradually dispersed to re-evaluate their odds.

Shortly after this I took my leave of H.M.S. York, and returned to base to obtain details of my next ship. Incidentally, throughout this book, the ships mentioned are only a few of those that I worked on during World War II which included vessels ranging from Motor Launches to Battleships.

After leaving H.M.S. York the QF guns on a number of escort vessels occupied my attention. Then came a half day,

F.7 - My wife Joyce and I, around August 1939

instructional visit to H.M.S. Marshall Soult, a 6,400 tons (approx. 6504 tonnes) monitor, being used as a 15" BL Gun, Turret Training Ship in Chatham Dockyard. Named after one of Napoleon's Generals, she was built at Palmer's Shipyard on the Tyne and served with the Dover Patrol in World War I.

Like most people who see the inside of a 15" gun turret for the first time, I was amazed at the size of everything and the engineering technology involved in operating the turret.

Shortly after this, wedding bells sounded when following a three year courtship, Miss Heather Joyce Luff and I were married at St Paul's Church, Chatham on 29th July 1939, the beginning of 64 years of married life (F.7). The service, which was fully choral, included the singing of the hymns "The voice that once over Eden" and "Handel's Largo".

Our wedding reception took place at the Navy House, Chatham, and among our wedding presents was an elegant clock, a gift from the members of the Afloat Party, every member of which received a piece of wedding cake in a small decorative box.

During this time, as the War clouds gathered over Europe, I found myself busy on destroyers of the Reserve Fleet that were at anchor, not too far apart in isolated reaches of the river.

Known as "dead ships" and with nobody aboard, they were in what was termed "a state of preservation" that required any upper deck metal work that was likely to go rusty to be painted or greased. The breech mechanisms and the bores of guns were thickly coated with grease, and canvass muzzle covers and large canvass covers laced up at the rear of the gun shield, provided further protection.

The ships were looked after by Royal Navy "Care and Maintenance Parties" who kept watch on the ships and ensured that all aboard was well and carefully preserved.

A small boat known as a "Trot Boat" operating from Gillingham Pier, near the Dockyard, transported my "mate" and I to and from the ships. Once aboard one of these destroyers it was rather an eerie sensation, to be in a remote stretch of the river with a rather old and bleak looking destroyer all to ourselves.

The guns were in the main 4" and 4.7" BL Guns in single low angle mountings. The first job was to "discover" the breach mechanism under its layer of thick grease. It was then stripped, degreased with plenty of paraffin oil, examined, reassembled, tested for correct function, and finally re-preserved with a lighter type of grease. This was to ensure that should the ships be recalled to service at short notice, as seemed likely, they would virtually be ready for use.

These precautions became necessary as Germany's aim to conquer Europe became more and more apparent. On 13th March 1938, Germany had annexed Austria and on 15th March 1939 occupied Czechoslovakia.

Then on the 15th August 1939, after it became clear that Poland would be the next victim of German aggression, the British Government signed a Treaty of Mutual Assistance with Poland.

Germany invaded Poland on Friday 1st September 1939 and on the 2nd September, Anglo-French ultimatums were sent to Germany urging her to withdraw her armed forces from Poland. The British ultimatum was due to expire at 9am on Sunday 3rd September and the one from France at 5pm.

On Sunday 3rd September 1939, as German forces continued to invade Poland and the Anglo-French ultimatums having expired, both France and Great Britain, supported by countries of the British Commonwealth, declared War on Germany and World War II had begun.

On the Sunday morning, of 3rd September 1939, when War broke out, I was busily employed aboard H.M.S. Worcester, a "W" Class destroyer built under the Emergency War Programme of 1915. She had a complement of 134 men and carried a main armament of four 4.7" BL guns in single mountings.

She lay alongside the wall of No. 3 Basin, close to where a lock gate system gave the Basin access to the R Medway.

An air of expectancy had hung over the ship all the morning, hopes still remaining that War could be avoided at the last minute. It was not to be however, and the deadline for peace having expired, the Prime Minister, Mr Neville Chamberlain, came on the radio and announced that the Nation was at War.

We had not long to wait for the first alarm for within what seemed like minutes after the Declaration of War; the air raid sirens gave forth into a dismal wailing sound. Acting on previous instructions, my mate and I in company with about twenty Dockyard men who were also working aboard, made our way down the ship's gangway, with as much dignity as we could muster, but slightly faster than usual.

Once ashore we dispersed to take shelter as best we could, with some of us crouching under the structure of a large dockside crane. Meanwhile it was all action on the "Worcester", fire hoses were run out from the ship to hydrants ashore, and the appropriate ship's stations manned.

After a short time the all clear sounded and with no signs of enemy aircraft and with sighs of relief, we all filed back aboard the ship to continue our work, amid a buzz of conversation.

During my time on the "Worcester" I met several naval reservists who had been recalled from "Civvy Street" where they had been employed by the Post Office, and during my lunch breaks I managed to repair the hinges on some of their navy issue, metal hat boxes, prized possessions of their previous service with the Royal Navy. This pleased them very much.

With the outbreak of War, a number of reservists employed in the Depot were recalled for active service, including several members of the Afloat Party, who took with them our best wishes for their safe return.

Around this time another ship to occupy my attention was

one of the paddle driven pleasure steamers requisitioned by the Admiralty for the duration of the War, mainly for minesweeping and anti-aircraft duties. The Local New Medway Steam Packet Company of Rochester, Kent, made its contribution, as announced in the Chatham, Rochester and Gillingham News for the 15th September 1939, which

stated: "All vessels of the New Medway Steam Packet Company have been requisitioned by the Admiralty. They are being prepared for various uses and the Royal Sovereign and the Royal Daffodil, the Company's latest luxury cross-channel boats have already departed and.". "In addition to this, many of the Company's Officers have been retained in the various ships and commissioned into the Royal Naval Reserve".

Other New Medway Steam Packet ships requisitioned were the Queen of Thanet, Queen of Kent and the Medway Queen. The Queen of Thanet was originally H.M.S. Melton, built for the Admiralty in 1916 as a minesweeper.

In the early 1930's The Queen of Thanet, while operating as a pleasure boat, ran one-day return trips from the Sun Pier Chatham to Calais in France, allowing passengers four hours ashore.

The "Eagle Line" on the R Thames also made its contribution to the Admiralty's needs, including the pleasure boats Royal Eagle and the Crested Eagle, which were converted for naval purposes and operated in the Thames estuary area.

One of the requisitioned paddle steamers, came into Chatham Dockyard, around this time, and I spent a couple of days or so checking her anti-aircraft armament, which was mounted on her spacious wooden upper deck. Her armament consisted of a number of 2 Pdr Mk II QF "Pom-Pom" guns, suitable for surface action and for use against low flying aircraft such as German aircraft engaged in coastal mine laying operations. Introduced into the Service in 1915, these guns were mainly used on auxiliary ships during World War II.

The 2 Pdr Mk II had a rate of fire of 200 rounds per minute, and originally the ammunition was fed to the gun by means of a 25 round fabric belt, but in later models a 114 round steel link belt came into use.

It was a "comfortable" gun to work on, as you simply raised a hinged lid, and the mechanism was readily available to work on. The job went well, and it was the only time that I worked on 2 Pdr Mk II QF guns, as they had a limited distribution.

Shortly after this I left Chatham Dockyard for a while on "detached duty" at Great Yarmouth in Norfolk, for the purpose of installing a gun on a fishing drifter, and attending gun trials at sea and Chapter 2 that follows gives an account of these duties.

CHAPTER 2

**Great Yarmouth, Norfolk and
The Fishing Drifter Rose Hilda**

October 1939 to January 1940

Around this time a number of fitters left the Gunwharf on "detached duty" which meant that they were not permanently transferred, but were due to return at an unspecified date. They were stationed at such ports as Liverpool, Hull and Newcastle-on-Tyne, where in addition to working on the guns of Naval vessels, they also dealt with the guns of Defensively Equipped Merchant ships (DEMs). Other fitters and other grades of Depot staff travelled further afield to serve at naval bases overseas.

In mid October 1939, as part of this general movement of staff, a Depot Notice appeared that invited applications for the posts of two Chargemen of Fitters on a "temporary acting basis" (surely no position ever hung on a more slender thread). One post was at Lowestoft in Suffolk and the other at Great Yarmouth in Norfolk, and in keeping with security regulations, no further details were given.

I submitted an application for one of the posts, and together with Frank Booty, a fellow gun fitter and close friend of mine, we were selected for the posts. Frank, a native of Lowestoft, had a preference for that town, so I settled for Great Yarmouth.

Prior to leaving, we had instructions on the type of gun we

would be dealing with, and also had the opportunity to strip and reassemble its breech mechanism. This was necessary, as the gun was no longer in widespread use with the Royal Navy and had been re-introduced for wartime service.

It was a 12 Pdr 12 cwt QF gun (F.8) and although introduced into the Royal Navy in December 1894, it was still an excellent weapon, having been used in World War I on various types of naval vessels, including submarines, and was also one of the earliest anti-aircraft guns.

The gun had a maximum range of 11,750 yards, (approx 6.68 miles) (10,744m) at an elevation of 40°.

It used brass cartridge case ammunition and had a relatively small breech mechanism that weighed 56 lbs (25 kg).

F.8 - A 12 Pdr 12 cwt Quick Firing gun, as fitted to the "Rose Hilda" (Photo: "Explosion" Museum of Naval Firepower, Gosport, Hants.)

My final instructions were to report to the Shipyard of Messrs Fellows and Son Ltd at Great Yarmouth. Messrs Fellows had the contract to manufacture and assemble a gun platform on the bow of a fishing boat, and then to secure the gun in its mounting to the platform. I was responsible for the gun and its breech mechanism and dealing with any problems with them that might arise during gun trials at sea.

So, feeling quite happy with the 12 Pdr, Frank and I

travelled from Chatham, via London, to Lowestoft, where after wishing him good luck I carried on to Great Yarmouth.

The town was completely "blacked out" when I arrived, late in the evening, with a somewhat urgent need to find accommodation for the night. Fortunately, after a short search, I managed to obtain accommodation in a small guest house that I liked on sight.

The middle aged lady that owned the guest house was a most pleasant and discerning lady, and we sat up well into the night, drinking cups of tea and exchanging views on the War, politics and life in general. At the end of which, despite my protests, she nominated me as the most individualistic person she had ever met. On this happy note and all in good humour, I thanked her for her mid night analysis, and retired to bed. Also looking back down the years, I think she was right.

F.9 - The "Rose Hilda" - the gun was fitted near to where the two members of the crew are standing (Photo: Great Yarmouth Museum, Norfolk)

I was up bright and early the next morning and rearing to go, so armed with directions from the lady of the guest house, I soon located Fellows' Shipyard on the R Yare.

Once inside the Shipyard's Main Office I met Mr Fellows, a most affable man, who informed me that the gun was to be installed on a fishing drifter named the "Rose Hilda" (F.9 & F.11). The gun had not arrived, but its high angle mounting, suitable for anti-aircraft work was out in the Yard. He then informed me that should I require accommodation, it could be arranged with a Mr & Mrs Hunt, who lived within the confines of the Boat Yard. An offer I quickly accepted. Among his other duties Mr Hunt was also caretaker of the Yard.

"The Rose Hilda" YM 93, was built at Fellows' Yard in 1930. She was built of steel with a net tonnage of 49 tons, and was powered by a 33 HP engine. Her owner, Mr William J E Green Ltd of Winterton, went to sea at the age of ten and became both a skipper and a boat owner. He also owned another drifter named the "Ocean Swell". The name drifter for these vessels was derived from the fact that while fishing, they drifted with the current.

As regards the Shipyard, it was rather small and dealt mainly with repairs to drifters, a number of which were in the Yard undergoing repairs. It possessed a small dry dock, with the unusual feature, that its sides were lined with well preserved baulks of timber.

Mr Hunt's house, my temporary residence, was well placed for viewing the Rose Hilda as she lay in the R Yare, which flowed past Fellows' Shipyard.

I also had a good look over the Rose Hilda where a

shipwright was busily engaged in constructing a large circular teak base near to the bow of the ship. It was to this base that the gun mounting would be bolted. This was not an easy job, as the decks of fishing drifters do not readily lend themselves to becoming gun platforms.

While waiting for the gun to arrive, an Admiralty order came through instructing me to proceed to Harwich in Essex, where a ship required attention to a gun. The vessel's number was given and the destination was an enclosed backwater in Harwich.

So, with a Royal Navy car as my transport, and accompanied by my ever faithful toolbox, I set off for Harwich. On arrival, the ship proved to be a red painted Trinity House Lightship, a rather unusual assignment.

I climbed aboard, to be greeted by the Lightship Keeper, who was expecting me, and we made our way to a working area where on a bench stood the lightship's firing apparatus (F.10).

F.10 - An impression of the firing apparatus aboard the Trinity House Lightship at Harwich in Essex

It was made of solid bronze with no moving parts and had a stout base, approximately 15" (375mm) square.

The apparatus was in fact a very small replica of the large artillery mortars of the 1856 period, which often weighed in the region of 5 tons (5.08 tonnes) and which were used to fire spherical shots and incendiary devices over the walls of fortifications and onto the decks of ships.

I gave the "small mortar" a thorough examination, checking it for sharp edges, cracks or any other faults and found no sign of anything that would make it dangerous to use and reported to the Keeper to this effect, and as it was a time of high security I never pursued the function of the mortar with the Keeper.

Later however, on consulting a book on ships, published in 1939, I found it contained the following reference to lightships:-

"In addition many lightships are equipped with apparatus for sending out submarine signals, these being picked up on instruments by liners", and there the matter rests.

Returning to the Royal Navy car, which had waited for me, we made our way back to Great Yarmouth, where I spent the rest of the evening catching up on my letter writing.

Meanwhile the gun had arrived at the local railway station, so the next morning, with the help of three or four muscular members of Messrs Fellows' Yard staff, equipped with stout lifting ropes, we manoeuvred the barrel from a railway truck into a lorry and conveyed it back to the Shipyard, where it quickly became the focus of attention.

Before finishing for the day, I unpacked the breech mechanism from its box, stripped it, and after a thorough examination, reassembled it, ready to be assembled to the gun.

At this stage the international laws of the sea came into operation in relation to the Rose Hilda and it was decreed, that as the gun was due to be mounted on the ship's bow, and therefore could be used offensively, the Rose Hilda must fly the Royal Navy Ensign.

In addition to this the civilian crew, consisting of three or four fishermen and the skipper, were required to be converted into uniformed members of the Royal Navy. So off they went to H.M.S. Pembroke, the shore based naval establishment at Chatham for a short course on the ways of the Royal Navy and to be fitted out with suits of navy blue.

I had a yarn with the crew, when they returned in their new uniforms and dancing for joy on the deck of the Rose Hilda, as they proudly displayed their bright tins of Navy issue tobacco, known throughout the Service as "Ticklers". This was a "nickname" derived from the fact that at one time "Ticklers" jam was issued to the Fleet in a similar type of tin.

By this time the teak base for the gun had been completed and the operation of installing the gun and its mounting aboard the Rose Hilda could proceed. For lifting purposes during this operation, an ancient, but very acceptable manually operated mobile crane had been borrowed from Messrs Crabtree, a neighbouring boat yard.

Operated manually, by means of various crank handles, the crane successfully lifted the gun into its mounting. The gun was then connected to the recoil and recuperating systems on the mounting and I assembled the breech mechanism to the gun.

It had been a busy day and had reached late afternoon by the time our mobile crane operated by its crank handles commenced to lift the gun and it's mounting onto the gently bobbing Rose Hilda.

We were all delighted as we watched the gun, attached to the hook of the crane by means of wire slings, swing out high over the R Yare towards its destination. Then it all happened as with a metallic clang and a desperate shudder of the jib, the crane gave up the ghost and the jib refused to move either towards the ship or towards the shore, leaving the gun dangling over the water of the river.

Come what may the jib could not be persuaded to move, and in order to avoid further trouble in the fast approaching darkness it was decided to secure the crank handles with ropes and leave any further action until daylight the following morning.

With a last lingering look at "my gun" I retired to Mrs Hunt's house nearby, where a nicely cooked meal of freshly caught herrings did much to revive my slightly jaded outlook.

My bedroom window gave a splendid view of the Rose Hilda and several times during the night I gazed out of the window to check on the welfare of the gun, as suspended from the crane, it swayed like a marionette in the freshening breeze. I also reflected a little on the most endearing phrases one would use if reporting back to the Gunwharf at Chatham that a 12 Pdr gun lay at the bottom of the R Yare.

In the morning fortune smiled on us, as the fault was located, rectified, and the mounting positioned on the gun platform without further incident. During the process of bolting the mounting to its teak base, however, the base distorted to such an extent that it proved impossible to train the mounting and it remained fixed in one position.

The design office and the engineering workshop at Fellows' Yard quickly went into action and produced a steel base plate that replaced the teak base and solved the problem.

Finally, training stops were fitted to the mounting in order to control the gun's "arc of fire" and prevent the gun firing into the ship's superstructure etc. A date was then set for gun trials at sea.

The morning of the trials was bitter cold, with an icy wind blowing, as I made my way aboard the Rose Hilda. Once aboard I met the Royal Naval Commander in charge of the trials and responsible for the subsequent report. He was a slightly built man in his mid fifties, who told me that he had been recalled for wartime duties, having served most of his time on battleships, a far cry indeed from our present position on a fishing drifter. The Commander and I went forward to check that the gun was all in order, and shortly after this, the ship left her moorings and headed downstream towards the mouth of the harbour.

On the way down the river we passed another drifter making her way up the river and a member of her crew shouted across to inform us that they had survivors aboard from a ship that had struck a mine just off the coast.

After leaving the calm of the harbour we entered the North Sea, where a heavy swell was running, so the Commander and I retreated to the galley in the stern of the ship, where a member of the crew had a cheery fire going and served us with large mugs of tea.

Heavy seas were the Rose Hilda's cue to perform some of her seagoing repertoire, which included rolling, pitching and at times almost standing on her stern. In this manner we arrived at the firing area and it was time for the Commander and I to leave the galley and make our way cautiously to the gun platform, to be joined by the gun's crew who took up their positions on the gun, ready for the trials to commence.

The actual trials consisted of firing a total of four rounds, one at full depression, one at maximum elevation and two at intermediate degrees of elevation. Being a QF gun the ammunition was of the brass cartridge case type, while for the purpose of trials, practice shells that did not explode were used.

So, with the gun's crew in position, and the gun platform swaying in all directions the trials got under way, while the Commander and I hung on to the safety rail surrounding the gun platform with one hand and did our best with the other hand to steady the seaman loading the gun.

The gun opened fire, with the ear-splitting crack peculiar to this type of gun and cordite fumes filled the air as the first round, at full depression, made a clean entry into the water. Further ear-splitting cracks and cordite fumes followed as the two intermediate rounds headed skywards.

Then came the forth and final round during which the maximum elevation of the gun coincided with a particular high lift of the bow. This resulted in the shell going upwards, directly above our heads which on the basis of "what goes up must come down" did not exactly endear us to the proceedings. Never-the-less, despite the adverse effect that the heaving seas had on the stability of the gun platform, the trial of the gun and its mounting were a success. Although it was clear the unstable conditions on the gun platform in rough weather would make accurate firing almost impossible.

Next, after the gun had been made secure and the empty

cases collected (to be reformed etc. at an Armament Depot for future use), we all departed from the gun platform. The gun's crew returned to their quarters or other duties, while the Commander and I returned to our haven in the galley to consume more piping hot mugs of tea as we made out way back to Great Yarmouth.

The Rose Hilda entered the smooth waters of the harbour in fine style and proceeded up the river to her berth alongside Fellows' Yard. Before going ashore I said cheerio to the ship's crew and thanked them for their assistance.

Once ashore, I took my leave of the Royal Naval Commander, wishing him well for the rest of the War, as he departed to prepare his report.

The next day it was time to say farewell to the good fisher folk of Great Yarmouth and return to H.M. Gunwharf Chatham. In the morning, after another excellent breakfast of fresh herrings, I thanked Mr & Mrs Hunt for their hospitality during my stay in their home and then made my way to the nearby main office, and having tendered my thanks to Mr Fellows and his staff for their excellent co-operation, I headed for Great Yarmouth railway station. On the way to the station I met the crew of the Rose Hilda, who gave me a boisterous and cheery send off.

On arriving back at Chatham I resumed my place as a fitter with the Afloat Party, together with my colleague Frank Booty, who had been successfully busy at Lowestoft on the drifter "Boy Phillip".

As a matter of interest, post war records show that the Rose

Hilda saw War Service as His Majesty's Drifter Rose Hilda. In 1954 she was sold to Lowestoft and renamed "Dawn Water" (LT90) and was scrapped in 1965 after 35 years service.

F.11 - The "Rose Hilda" in rough seas
(Photo: Great Yarmouth Museum, Norfolk)

CHAPTER 3

Armament Work in H.M. Dockyard Chatham

5th January 1940 to 31st June 1942

This Chapter covers a period of 2½ years spent in Chatham Dockyard working on the guns of most types of Royal Navy vessels, with the exception of battleships, which were too large to enter the Dockyard.

The Dockyard covered an area of 396acres (F.12), and during World War II employed a maximum workforce of 13,000, of whom 2,000 were women. It also had a single-decker bus service and its own internal railway system.

The year 1940 proved to be a year of great anxiety and bravery, as after the fall of France on the 22nd June 1940, Great Britain, the British Empire and members of the Free Allied Forces fought to stop the mighty German war machine as it spread death and destruction across Europe. The War at sea also intensified as German "U" Boats" and surface raiders took a heavy toll of merchant ships and their crews.

The Dockyard was kept extremely busy, both repairing and building ships, and the Afloat Party serviced guns in almost every part of the Dockyard, and following work on a series of ships, I was detailed to service the gun on H.M. Submarine Salmon (F.14) which had arrived in the Dockyard, around the end of March 1940.

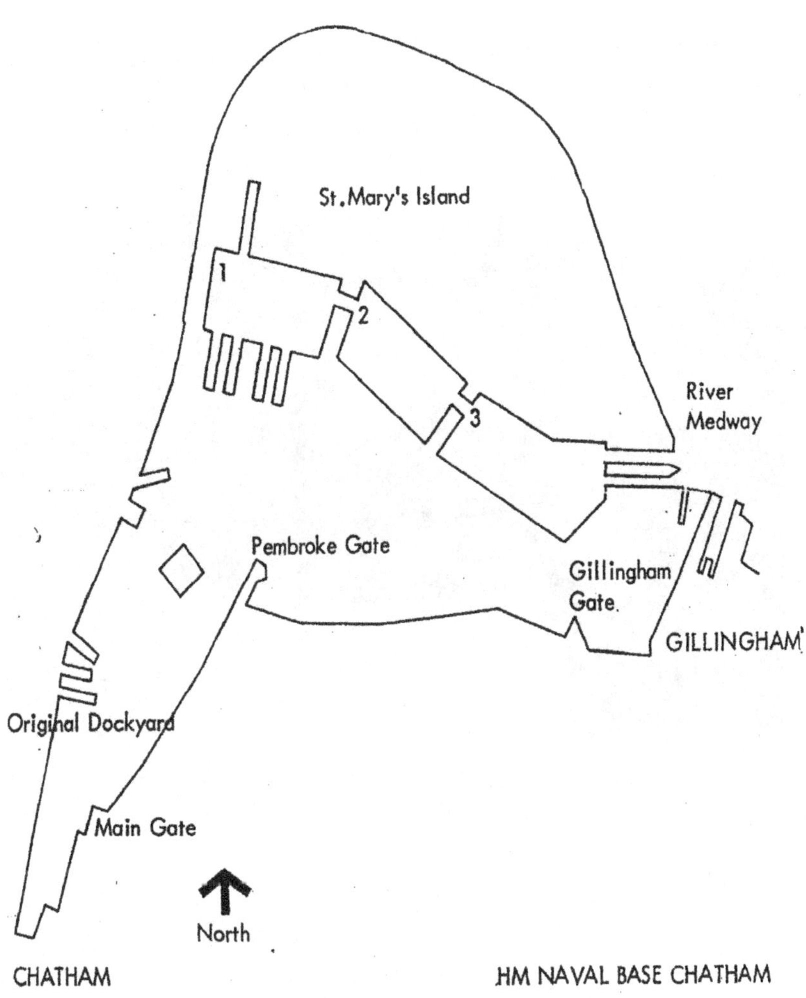

F.12 - Map of the H.M. Dockyard, Chatham, showing Basins 1, 2 and 3 and the Dry Docks (From: Chatham Dockyard Historical Society, Kent)

She "tied up" in one of the large Basins, in what was known as "Battery Corner", near to the Battery Sheds, where the batteries used by the submarines were either recharged or replaced. In the same area was the "lay apart" store that accommodated items removed from the submarine while Dockyard work was in progress, and when I arrived at the ship's gangway a member of the crew was coming up the gangway with a Lewis Gun on his shoulder, to be deposited in the store.

F.13 - The Main Gate of H.M. Dockyard, Chatham
The Main Gate was built in 1720

F.14 - H.M.S. Salmon, a 670 ton submarine, armed with one 3" 20 cwt QF Gun and six 21" Torpedo Tubes (Photo: Royal Naval Museum, H.M Naval Base, Portsmouth)

The gun on H.M.S. Salmon was a 3" 20 cwt QF gun, introduced into the Service in March 1914, and specially designed for anti-aircraft work. It had a vertically sliding breech block and a maximum range of 12,920 yards at 40° (approx 7.34 miles) (11,810m).

During World War I the gun was used extensively by the Army and Navy and in World War II was the standard gun on "S" and "U" Classes of submarines.

I spent a couple of days on H.M.S. Salmon stripping and examining the gun, while working on the restricted space of the gun platform.

On the last day, an Examiner of Naval Ordnance came aboard and "passed out" the gun.

As a matter of interest, in relation to H.M.S. Salmon the patrol she carried out from the 2nd to 16th December 1939, while under the command of Lieutenant Commander E O Bickford, was regarded by the Admiralty as one of the most outstanding submarine patrols of World War II, and the following account is based on the official report.

During the patrol H.M.S. Salmon launched torpedo attacks on German Naval vessels on two separate occasions, sinking a "U" boat on the 4th December 1939 and badly damaging two cruisers on the 13th December 1939.

In between these two events and at 09.30 hours on the 12th December she sighted the German liner "Bremen" at a range of 2,000 yards, speeding on her way back to Germany.

The submarine surfaced and in accordance with the rules of the sea signalled the "Bremen" to stop.

When the "Bremen" failed to stop and sped on her way, the

order was given to fire a warning shot ahead of her, but just as the gun layer was about to fire, a Dornier DO18 appeared, and the gun platform was cleared, as the submarine was forced to dive. Also, in accordance with the laws of the sea, no attempt was made by H.M.S. Salmon to torpedo the "Bremen", a decision endorsed by the Admiralty.

Work on the guns of frigates and destroyers also occupied my attention during the first three months of 1940, and when the "H" class destroyers, "Havoc", "Hostile" (F.15) and "Hotspur" came into the Dockyard for repairs, I was detailed to work on the 4.7 " QF guns of two of them.

F.15 - H.M.S. Hostile formed part of the British 2nd Destroyer Flotilla at the 1st Battle of Narvik in Norway, on the 10th of April 1940 (Photo: Royal Naval Museum, H.M. Naval Base, Portsmouth)

Not long after this, on the 10th April 1940, these three destroyers took part in the 1st Battle of Narvik in Norway, one of the Royal Navy's engagements during the Norwegian Campaign of March to June 1940.

In this campaign Great Britain and her Allies tried without success, to prevent Germany occupying Norway.

Together with the destroyers H.M.S. Hardy and H.M.S. Hunter, they formed the British 2nd Destroyer Flotilla which under the command of Captain B A W Warburton Lee, in H.M.S. Hardy, sailed up the fjords leading to Narvik and launched a devastating surprise attack on German Naval Units occupying the port of Narvik.

As a result of the engagement, the Germans lost two destroyers sunk, three destroyers badly destroyed and a supply ship blown up.

The British Forces lost two destroyers H.M.S. Hardy beached and H.M.S. Hunter sunk.

The powerful main armament of the "H" class destroyers consisted of four 4.7" QF guns in single mountings, fitted with gun shields. The gun had a maximum range of 16,970 yards at 40° (approx. 9.4 miles) (15.516m) and fired a 50 lb (22.68kg) shell.

Like a number of other types of QF guns the 4.7" QF gun was known as a semi- automatic gun. This indicated that the breech mechanism could be operated entirely manually or be switched to "semi-automatic" in which the breech block would open and close automatically. In opening automatically the spent brass cartridge case was forcibly ejected.

On occasions, with QF guns of this type, "Slip Tests" were held, in order to test the recoil system etc. of the mounting and the guns semi-automatic function. These tests did not occur very often, but during World War II, I attended five or so, all of them in Chatham Dockyard.

The test was quite spectacular, and was attended by a Naval Ordnance Examiner, members of the Dockyard Gun

Mounting Section, including the Gun Mounting Section's "heavy duty squad", who operated the "slip gear" used in the test, and following is an account of a "slip test" that I participated in.

In preparation for the test, and with the breech mechanism in manual, I loaded an empty brass cartridge case into the gun, and then set the breech mechanism for semi-automatic function.

Next, the heavy duty squad went into action and connected one end of the slip gear to the rear end of the gun barrel, and the other end to a special steel shackle, let into the deck of the ship, and positioned so as to take the heavy duty squad well clear of the rear of the gun.

The heavy duty squad then showed their muscle power, and by means of a lever that operated the slip gear, pulled the gun back to its fully recoiled position, and secured the slip gear in this position by means of a quick release, chain, slip link. A gun mounting fitter then set the semi-automatic pawl on the gun mounting to its operating position, and we both rejoined the group, assembled a safe distance to the side of the gun.

Then, at a given signal from the Naval Ordnance Examiner, a member of the heavy duty squad, using a hammer, knocked the quick release link off the slip gear and the slip gear fell away from the gun.

On being released, the gun, after a shuddering start, moved rapidly forward as it "ran out" to take up its normal position. During the "run out" the pawl on the mounting activated the breech mechanism, causing the breech block to fly open and strike a set of extractors that forcibly ejected the empty brass cartridge case. The case sailed through the air and hit the deck with a resounding clang.

It now remained to test the breech block for semi-automatic closing.

So, with the breech block held open by the "hooks" on two spring loaded extractors, while at the same time a powerful coiled spring, contained in the lever that opened and closed the breech, was exerting pressure to close the breech block, the empty cartridge case was once more, carefully manually loaded into the gun.

As the case was pushed home, it forced the "hooks" on the extractor, clear of the breech block and activated by the coiled spring, the breech block, travelling at a frightening speed, slammed home to its closed position.

Finally, both the gun mounting and the breech mechanism were reset to manual operation and I unloaded the empty cartridge case to bring the test to an end.

Thus, with another "slip test" successfully and safely completed, we made our way ashore, with the heavy duty squad and their equipment bringing up the rear.

Following closely on the events in Norway, the British Expeditionary Force

(B E F) and the French Army were fighting for their very survival against the fierce onslaught of German Forces invading France.

Under extreme pressure the B E F was forced back onto the French channel port of Dunkirk and in order to save the B E F from complete destruction it was decided that every effort should be made to evacuate the B E F and return it to England.

The evacuation of the B E F from Dunkirk which lasted from 27th May to 4th June 1940, was an epic of World War II, and resulted in 338,225 members of the

B E F being returned safely to Great Britain.

During this time, Chatham Dockyard concentrated its vast expertise and resources on destroyers and other ships that were engaged in the Dunkirk operation, including those leaving the Yard and those coming in for repairs after being damaged. The badly damaged ships were quickly placed in dry dock, before any underwater damage could cause further complications.

One of my tasks on a number of the damaged ships was to go aboard, immediately after they had been docked and to check if the ship's main armament guns had been damaged in a manner that would make it dangerous to lift them out of their mountings.

Among the Naval vessels undergoing repairs in Chatham Dockyard around this time was the ship H.M.S. Pelican on which I had worked back in 1939, when she was a spick and span new addition to the Fleet.

But as I looked down at her from the roadway above her dry dock, she bore all the marks of War, with her stern decking blasted wide open and rolled back like a piece of carpet. Another badly damaged ship in dry dock about this time was the destroyer H.M.S. Ivanhoe.

Among the outgoing destroyers that I worked on during the Dunkirk period was the Flotilla Leader H.M.S. Keith, berthed in a quiet secluded corner of the Dockyard. Having completed the work on the guns, I was packing up my tools ready to depart, when the ship's Chief Ordnance Artificer came up and enquired how things were going.

We had a chat about the guns for a little while, and then, wishing him all the very best, I took my leave.

A few days later, however, I was walking along one of the roads in the Dockyard, when who should I meet but the Chief Ordnance Artificer of H.M.S. Keith. We passed the time of day, and had a conversation, during which in keeping with the wartime slogan "Careless Talk Costs Lives" I refrained from asking questions, but later learned that H.M.S. Keith had been lost at Dunkirk.

After the Dunkirk Evacuation, the War came a little closer to Britain, as Germany tried, unsuccessfully to destroy the Royal Air Force and its aerodromes, during the Battle of Britain (1st July to 31st October 1940), which was the forerunner of the "Blitz" (7th September 1940 to 10th May 1941) when Germany attempted to defeat Britain and her Allies by means of prolonged bombing raids on Service targets and the civilian population.

Like many other places at this time, the skies over the Chatham area were criss-crossed with white vapour trails and the sound of distant machine gun fire came through the air as the Battle of Britain took place overhead, while on occasions a Spitfire or a Hurricane flew low over the scene to perform a "victory roll".

On one occasion, a group of us watched, in disbelief as a German plane glided, silently, just above mast height, across one of the large water basins in Chatham Dockyard, and slowly disappeared into the distance. The pilot was clearly visible, sitting up straight and looking straight ahead. We learned later that the plane had landed on a hill, the other side of nearby Strood.

Also around this time, I spent a week or so working on ships out in the R Medway, where the broad expanse of the vapour trials was clearly visible and during this time, while three of us were travelling downstream in a small wooden motor boat, the close proximity of machine gun fire, caused us to take a sudden dive to the bottom of the boat, where we remained hunched up until things had quietened down a bit.

Sometime later, after returning ashore, I answered a call from a small unit of the Royal Artillery. Their gun was sited in an area of the Dockyard, known as the "Bulls Nose" where a set of lock gates connected the Dockyard to the R Medway.

It was a small calibre QF gun, with a sliding breech block, and I stripped, examined and reassembled the mechanism and carried out a series of functional tests and found the gun in excellent condition. I reported accordingly to the soldier in charge, and then said cheerio to this group of soldiers who were playing their part in defending Chatham Dockyard.

As the Battle of Britain (1st July to 31st October 1940) drew to a close, the "Blitz" (7th September 1940 to 10th May 1941) in all its fury was launched by Germany on "war targets" and the civilian population of the United Kingdom.

Night after night Royal Artillery anti-aircraft guns opened fire on German bombers, either attacking the Chatham district or passing close by on their way to bomb London.

On several occasions at the beginning of the "Blitz" and in broad daylight, extremely large numbers of German bombers, escorted by hordes of fighter planes, flew close to the Chatham area on their way to bomb London.

These massive formations of enemy aircraft were indeed a frightening sight to the many people viewing them from the ground. The Royal Air Force and members of the Allied Air

Forces, however, although suffering serious losses themselves, took a deadly toll of such formations.

Early in the War, my wife Joyce became a volunteer member of the Borough of Chatham, Air Raid Precautions (A R P) Service and we often said good morning on the doorstep as Joyce came off night duty and I set off for a day shift in the Dockyard.

During the "Blitz" my wife Joyce was a member of the rescue team that attended the scene, when at 11.32am on Saturday 5th October 1940, high explosive bombs devastated the Ordnance Street and Rochester Street areas of Chatham, killing 8 people and injuring 23. Joyce also took part in other dangerous incidents.

F.16 - H.M.S. Arethusa, a cruiser that helped to defend the Chatham area during the air raids of August and October 1940 (Photo: Royal Naval Museum, H.M. Naval Base, Portsmouth)

Around this time the 5,220 ton cruiser H.M.S. Arethusa (F.16) was in Chatham Dockyard from the 7th August 1940 to 14th October 1940 undergoing repairs etc. and I was detailed to work on her eight 4" MK XVI QF anti-aircraft guns.

H.M.S. Arethusa was laying in No. 8 dry dock, the largest in the Dockyard, with her keel firmly supported on blocks at the bottom of the dock, and her sides "shored up", by large baulks of timber, secured between both sides of the ship and the sides of the Dock.

It was in this condition that during the "Blitz" H.M.S. Arethusa carried out one of the most unusual and somewhat hazardous exercises in Naval Gunnery: she opened fire, night after night, with her powerful 4" Mk XVI QF anti-aircraft guns, joining the Royal Artillery barrage in defence of the Chatham area and firing at bombers headed for London.

I was also told, at a later date, that during the firing, shipwrights and other members of the Dockyard staff were on duty at the dry dock, in order to ensure that the supporting "shores" etc. remained securely in position.

H.M.S. Arethusa had been firing for several nights before I joined her, and it was still essential that her guns received their scheduled overhaul before she went to sea again.

My instructions were to report to the Gunnery Officer, and not to the Chief Ordnance Artificer, as was my normal practice and to fit my work in with the Gunnery Officer's requirements,

On arriving aboard, about 8 o'clock, one morning, I was directed to the Officers' Mess, to be met by the Gunnery Officer, a true blue, in the best tradition of the Royal Navy. He was wearing his hat at an "Admiral Beatty" angle and despite having had a harrowing night manning the guns he greeted me in a most cordial manner, including the offer of a gin and tonic.

The Gunnery Officer explained his requirements and it was arranged that he would nominate the mounting to be worked on, and I would report back when it was completed to receive my next nomination.

In this fashion I gradually worked by way through the guns, often arriving in the morning to find a few empty cartridge cases still lingering in the ship's scuppers.

So after a very privileged experience and with all the guns complete I reported back to the indomitable Gunnery Officer and after wishing him well for the future, took my leave of H.M.S. Arethusa.

The 4" Mk XVI QF was probably the finest and most popular Royal Navy anti-aircraft gun of World War II. A total of 2,555 were manufactured and widely distributed throughout the Fleet. They were assembled in twin gun mountings, in which the twin guns were trained and elevated together, as a unit.

Other details were as follows:-

Weight of gun - 1 ton 17 cwt 23 lbs (approx. 1,860 kg).

Weight of Breech Mechanism - 3 cwt (approx. 150 kg).

Maximum Range - 19,850 yards at 45° (18,150m) (approx 11.3 miles).

They fired fixed ammunition and the shell weighed 35 lbs.

In July 1940, the Local Defence Volunteers, formed on 14th May 1940, were renamed the Home Guard and I became a private in a unit of the Chatham Home Guard, attached to the Royal West Kent Regiment, with our headquarters at the Territorial Drill Hall in Boundary Road, Chatham.

I attended as many parades as working in the evenings and weekends allowed and also attended one or two exercises, including an all night deployment, and a "mock" battle, against an enemy concealed in a "bombed out" area of the town.

In another exercise, that proved to be a rather humorous affair, we were treated to a demonstration of the "Indian Crawl". Although the "Indian Crawl" was required to be performed slowly, it was a splendid method of concealed crawling, as the body remained flat on the ground throughout the movement.

It did, however, call for a certain degree of fitness and agility on the part of the demonstrator, as at one stage the bent legs were alternatively extended sideways, in a somewhat frog like manner.

Unfortunately, the demonstrator was no agile "Red Indian" being in fact the manager of a local gentleman's outfitters, who was officially appointed as an officer, but self appointed as a "Red Indian". He was over six feet tall, weighted around 14 stone, and was very wooden and ungainly in his movements, while the baggy fitting Home Guard uniform belied his gentlemen's outfitters background.

About 100 of us lined the field to watch the demonstration. The field was covered in grass, about 2'6" high, and after a brief explanation of the exercise, he strode to the centre of the field and disappeared beneath the grass.

The enterprise was doomed to failure from the start, as with his large build and awkward movements, he proceeded across the field in the playful manner of a porpoise swimming through the water, with his posterior appearing first above the grass and then disappearing beneath it with each forward movement.

It was all too much for the assembled onlookers who burst into laughter and then joined together in a chorus of "we can see yer, we can see yer", accompanied by less complimentary remarks.

This was more than our would-be "invisible man" could stand; he climbed out of the grass, fully appreciating the humour of the situation and we all moved on to the next part of the exercise.

One of my activities at work, during this period, was associated with the Home Guard, and I spent several days at the Gunwharf, gauging the bores of Long Lee Enfield, 303 rifles for wear.

Those that came within the required limits were allocated for Home Guard use.

The Long Lee Enfield 303 rifle came into Service in November 1895 and was used in the Boer War (1899-1902) and during the early part of World War I (1914-1918).

It was gradually superseded by the Short Lee Enfield 303 Mk III rifle, adopted in 1907, to become Britain's standard service rifle during World War II (1939-1945).

One particular call out that I attended, came from a small steamer that required her gun to be checked. She was laying outside the Dockyard, in the R Medway, near to Strood Pier.

On arriving at the Pier, the ship proved to be a tramp steamer type of vessel, armed with a single 12 Pdr QF anti-aircraft gun. I hailed the ship and very soon a member of the crew rowed out to the Pier and took me out to the ship.

I was a bit taken back by the somewhat assorted attire favoured by the rower. It was however, but a foretaste of the clothes worn by the other five or six members of the crew who greeted me when I climbed aboard.

They were dressed in a wide range of colours displayed by woollen hats, neck scarves, jersey sweaters and assorted footwear.

As I started work on the gun, the crew gathered round the gun mounting and watched me at work for ten minutes or so, and then after a little good humoured banter they departed from the scene.

All went well with the job, and towards late afternoon, I contacted the "skipper" in his cabin, and let him know that the gun was in a serviceable condition and ready for use.

At this stage he asked me to report that he would like the gun and its mounting removed from the ship.

On returning to base I reported the "skipper's" request, and was instructed to return to the ship the next morning and inform him, that the removal of the gun and the mounting were a matter for discussion between the ship's owners and the Admiralty.

Unfortunately, I never delivered the message, for to my astonishment, when I arrived at Strood Pier the next morning, the ship had been sunk and there she was with only part of her funnel showing above the water. So I made my way back to Chatham Dockyard and reported that I had not been able to deliver my message as the ship was sunk.

Other work on guns took place in H.M.S. Pembroke, Chatham, one of the Royal Navy's shore based establishments. H.M.S. Pembroke was made up of numerous buildings etc.

which included a Royal Naval Barracks, a large Parade Ground, a Gunnery School and a Saluting Gun Base, and the whole establishment was adjoined to Chatham Dockyard.

The work I carried out took the form of routine checks on the guns in H.M.S. Pembroke's Gunnery School and those on the Saluting Gun Base.

The Gunnery School, that opened in 1908, was an oblong shaped building, with apertures in its walls, that allowed certain of the gun barrels to protrude outside the building and to be trained and elevated to a limited degree.

Various types of BL and QF guns were installed in the school, but in certain cases - the 15" BL gun for example - the barrel could not be accommodated in its entirety. In these cases, a short "sawn off" portion of the rear end of the barrel, with its breech mechanism assembled to it, was securely mounted on a stand and used for training purposes.

The Gunnery Classes were conducted by Royal Navy Officers and Petty Officer Gunnery Instructors, known as GIs. The GIs wore distinctive white gaiters and a tradition of the Gunnery School, was that Royal Navy personnel proceeding across the forecourt of the school, did so "at the double", although a brisk trot seemed to be sufficient.

During a gun drill, the clear precise orders of the GI guided the "gun's crew" throughout the exercise, and he also sorted out any mistakes that occurred. The further expertise of the Officers and the GIs soon became apparent when a class was assembled around the breech end of a gun to be instructed on other gunnery matters, including the manner in which the breech mechanism operated.

Questions from members of the class were always carefully

dealt with, while sound advice on the then current aspects of naval warfare was also included in the overall instructions.

My work on those guns not in use took place while the classes were in progress and therefore was required to be carried out quietly and unobtrusively. The breech mechanisms were subjected to pretty robust treatment during training sessions and part of my job was to remove any sharp edges or burrs that could cause cuts or damage to hands.

All moving parts of the breech mechanism were checked to ensure they worked correctly and smoothly, so as to avoid hold ups during demonstrations. In addition to this any "scores" or grooves on breech screw threads etc were "blended in" by using a small triangular section carborundum stone, a job that required patience.

At one time the mighty 15" BL "sawn off" gun received my attention in a similar manner, but none of its heavy components were stripped down.

During "stand easy" times, or when classes were over, I managed to exchange views and information on guns with a number of the GIs. It was also, indeed a privilege to witness, yet anther aspect of how the Royal Navy prepared for War.

The Saluting Base, with its Battery of three 3 Pdr QF Hotchkiss guns (F.17) was situated near to the Gunnery School, in a position overlooking the Parade Ground.

Hotchkiss guns, of various calibres were invented and manufactured by Mr Benjamin Hotchkiss, an American, born in Watertown, Connecticut, USA, in 1826.

In 1875 he established a factory at Dennis on the outskirts of Paris, and around 1884 the manufacture of Hotchkiss guns commenced in England, at the Newcastle-on-Tyne plant of Sir William Armstrong.

F.17 - A 3 Pdr Hotchkiss QF Saluting Gun

The 3 Pdr QF Hotchkiss gun was introduced into the Royal Navy service on the 7th September 1885.

I serviced the guns of the "Pembroke" Saluting Battery several times during the War, and on one occasion was called out to a rather unusual happening, in which someone had fired the gun, when it was not loaded, and the front portion of the firing pin had broken off and disappeared.

It was, however, common practice to fire this type of gun while it was unloaded and I had never met, or heard of any untoward results arising from this.

Having discussed the problem with the Officer-In-Charge of the Battery, I stripped the breech mechanism and located the missing part of the firing pin up the bore of the gun. I then carried out a routine check, fitted a new firing pin and reassembled the breech mechanism.

So, feeling quite happy with things, I took a firm grip on the gun's firing pistol, and pulled the trigger and "Hey Presto!" another firing pin top flew up the bore of the gun.

Then in order to check if the firing pins varied in any way, I fitted a third pin and pulled the trigger, with similar results as before.

At this stage the Assistant Foreman of factory, from Chatham Gunwharf came into the picture and tests were carried out on a number of firing pins and the gun's firing spring and they were found to be "correct to plan".

All our efforts were of no avail, and our final recommendations to the Officer in Charge were in the nature of a preventive measure, to be used when firing the gun in the unloaded position.

It required the person firing the gun to take a firm hold on the gun's re-cocking lever and to ease the striker, with its firing pin, slowly forward. This allowed the force of the firing spring to be gradually released, instead of "snapping" forward in the normal manner.

Strangely enough, however, in 1982 while I was researching some historical documents at Priddy's Hard Museum, at Gosport, Hampshire, in aid of my book "The History of the Royal Naval Armaments Depot, Priddy's Hard, Gosport, 1768-1977" published in 1997, I came across, by chance a War Department Memo dated 2 August 1890 that described a solution to the problem of broken firing pins on 6 Pdr and 3 Pdr QF Hotchkiss guns (App. 6 refers).

It was indeed a surprise to find this 1890 memo dealing with a problem that I met in the 1940s.

In 1890, when the memo was issued, the Hotchkiss QF guns, with their rapid rate of fire, were of prime importance as part of the Royal Navy's defence against attacks by fast moving Torpedo Boats.

Prior to, and during World War II, a battery of 3 Pdr Hotchkiss QF Saluting Guns were usually carried by battleships and cruisers for saluting purposes.

The time of the firing of each blank cartridge case during a salute is 5 seconds. All Salutes are in odd numbers, with the maximum of a 21 gun salute for Royal and National occasions. The number of firings for other salutes varies from 19 to 7, as laid down in the Queen's Regulations for the Royal Navy.

Back in the Dockyard, work on destroyers, with their powerful main armament of eight 4.7" QF guns, in twin gun mountings, occupied my time.

The twin guns, which were trained and elevated together, as a unit, had a range of 16,970 yards (15,520m), 9.64 miles. They fired a 50 lb (22.6k) shell.

Around 1938 and 1939, sixteen Tribal Class Destroyers came into service, with such names as "Ashanti", "Bedouin", "Eskimo" and "Mohawk".

I carried out examinations and overhauls etc. on the 4.7" QF guns of at least five Tribal Class destroyers, followed by the usual "pass out" by a Naval Ordnance Examiner.

In addition to their armament of guns and torpedoes, destroyers, in common with many other types of naval vessels, also carried Depth Charge Throwers (DCTs) (F.18), one of the Royal Navy's most formidable anti-submarine weapons of World War I and II.

Designed and manufactured by Messrs Thornycroft, the well known engineers, the first Depth Charge Throwers came into service around 1916, during World War I, and a total of 3,000 were supplied to the Royal Navy. They had a range of 40 yards (37m).

The DCTs were normally positioned one on each side of the ship in the afterpart of the ship, while on the stern of some vessels there was a launching rack from which Depth Charges could be released over the stern.

I spent a considerable amount of time in Chatham Dockyard engaged on overhauling both the Mk II and Mk IV type of Depth Charge Throwers and modifying the MK IVs and on one occasion taking part in a most unusual test involving a Depth Charge Thrower aboard a destroyer.

The test took place, in the confines of the Dockyard, on a destroyer berthed in one of the large basins. It was conducted under naval control, with members of the ship's company assisting.

My function was to "standby", and only take action if anything went wrong with the Depth Charge Thrower, which I had thoroughly checked the day before.

I was also informed that part of the test was to measure the deflection that occurred in the deck when the Depth Charge Thrower was fired. I must add, however, that firing even a dummy Depth Charge in the close confines of the Dockyard, had a strange air about it.

So with everyone in position the test got underway. First a

dummy Depth Charge, filled with concrete, and of the same weight and dimensions as a real Charge was loaded to the Thrower.

Then a thick rope was neatly coiled up on the deck, with one end of it secured aboard the ship. The other end was passed through a swivel pulley on one of the ship's davits and then secured to the dummy charge, through a hole, passing lengthwise through its centre.

At this stage a live cartridge was loaded into the explosive chamber of the Thrower, and with everyone standing well clear of the coiled rope, the Depth Charge Thrower was fired.

Away went the dummy Depth Charge, describing a perfect arc, as with the rope trailing behind it, it sped high over the waters of the basin, to disappear beneath its surface.

A team of 5 or 6 sailors then took up the rope, and working in unison, they ran along the deck, hauling in as they went, to bring the dummy charge, shedding streams of water, back into view, and finally hauling it aboard.

With the test completed I returned to base, to report that the trial had gone well.

Chatham Dockyard, with its high reputation for building and repairing submarines, had a regular requirement for submarine guns to be serviced.

The two main submarine guns were the 3" QF 20 cwt, used chiefly on the smaller submarines, while the 4" QF Mk XII, known as the "standard" submarine gun, was specially manufactured to a simplified design to allow for its immersion in water.

It had a horizontally sliding breech block with no semi

automatic gear, and was percussion firing only, and although of a simplified design, the breech mechanism weighed 2 cwt.

The gun had a maximum range of approximately 5.93 miles, at an elevation 20° and fired a 35 lb (15.88 kg) shell.

Gun trials on submarines, also took place at sea, and during the course of World War II, I attended, 3 or 4 such trials, going aboard the submarines at Sheerness, and following is a brief account of one that I attended, on a submarine that carried a 3" QF 20 cwt gun.

The days proceedings started early in the morning, at Gillingham Pier, near to the Dockyard, where a Naval Ordnance Examiner and myself boarded a boat, that took us the 9 miles or so down the R Medway to where the submarine was laying at the mouth of the river, off Sheerness.

F.18 - A Depth Charge Thrower

On arrival, the boat edged its way alongside the submarine, allowing us to climb carefully and gingerly aboard, by means of a narrow footplate and a handrail that skirted the coming tower.

After meeting the Petty Officer in charge of the gun's crew, we made our way to the gun platform and visually examined the gun's breech mechanism and operated it several times. The gun had already been declared all clear for trials.

We then made our way down below, and as the submarine got under way, we settled down in a small compartment, to sit and wait until we reached the firing area.

On reaching the firing area, we mustered on the gun platform, in company with the Petty Officer and the gun's crew, who took up their positions on the gun.

Then, under the overall direction of the Naval Ordnance Examiner, three rounds were fired. One round at full depression, and two at various degrees of elevation.

So, with no problems arising, the gun trial drew to a successful conclusion, and as the gun's crew gathered up the empty cartridge cases, and secured the gun, we made a final check of the gun and then went below to sit in our compartment.

The submarine made its way back to the Sheerness area, where we transferred to a small boat that transported us to Sheerness Dockyard.

The day concluded with a boat journey back to Gillingham Pier, during which time I reflected on another gun trial, safely and successfully conducted.

Also, living as I did about a mile from the Gunwharf, I was called out on several occasions on gun work requiring immediate attention.

One such occasion arose early one Sunday morning, when the Depot van arrived at our house, and the driver passed on the instruction that I was to proceed to Sheerness Dockyard, where out in the river a submarine required its gun to be serviced.

So, having called for my "fitter's mate", who also lived nearby, from his home, and collected my tool box from Chatham Dockyard, we sped by van to Sheerness Dockyard. On arriving at the Dockyard's Shipping Office, I had to assure the man in charge that our journey out into the estuary was really necessary, before he allocated a small boat to take us out to the submarine. He explained that reports had come through, that during the night, enemy aircraft had laid mines in the estuary, and in the interest of everybody's safety, boat movements were being kept down to a minimum, and boats' crews were working to a roster, each boat taking its turn.

Once aboard the submarine I reported to the Commanding Officer, who like many submarine Commanders during World War II, was a relatively young man, very casually dressed, as was then the custom with submarine personnel.

My "mate" and I then made our way to the gun platform, where a bitter cold wind coming in off the North Sea was making things uncomfortable.

The gun, a 3" QF 20 cwt gun, with a vertically sliding breech block, required the usual strip, examine etc. routine.

Work on the gun went very well indeed and had reached its final stages of reassembly. The last major component to be reassembled was a steel block that prevented the breech block falling out on to the deck when the breech was opened. The steel block was held in place by a small steel pin which after being inserted and rotated held the steel block in position.

Unfortunately, as I inserted the pin it slipped from my cold fingers and described three perfect arcs of a circle as it bounced down the outer casing of the submarine and disappeared into the R Medway.

All of a sudden I felt a feeling of nausea at the thought of telling the Commander the position on his gun. I waited five minutes in order to digest the loss of the pin and then related the incident to the Commander.

He took it all in his stride, without any adverse comments, which I much appreciated, and detailed a rating to go with me and check the gun's spares for a replacement.

A spare pin was not available, so the Commander sent a signal to Chatham Gunwharf, requesting a replacement pin, while my "mate" and I sat down below to await its arrival.

The pin arrived by van and boat transport in a remarkable short space of time, and with an inward sigh of relief, I pushed the pin home and rotated it into the locked position.

I then thanked the Commander for his assistance, and my "mate" and I set off for home by boat and train.

When working on the small platform of submarine guns, the danger of losing a part of the breech mechanism over the side was always a matter of constant concern.

I also made a short acquaintance with two USA naval vessels. One entered the Dockyard in a damaged condition, and while it was still in the lock entrance to the Dockyard, I was detailed to meet her and lend any assistance required on her guns.

After hailing an officer on the upper deck, from my position on the dockside, I was informed that help was not required, and following a few humorous exchanges with a couple of the ship's company, who were urging me "to give us the tools, and we will do the job", I retired from the scene.

The other vessel was one of the 50, old type USA destroyers received by Great Britain as a result of a Lease Lend agreement signed with the USA on the

3rd September 1940. In return for the destroyers the USA was granted long term leases on British bases in Newfoundland and the West Indies.

The destroyers were a very welcome addition to the Royal Navy, as at that time there was a pressing need for destroyers on Convoy duties etc.

I spent a full day on the destroyer, familiarising myself with her main armament in case of future need, but it proved to be the only one of the 50 destroyers that I spent any time on.

A happy event took place on the 23rd January 1942, when my wife Joyce gave birth to our son Richard, at the Royal Naval and Royal Marine Maternity Nursing Home, the Nore, Barnsole Road, Gillingham, Kent, under the care of that excellent lady, Matron I S Stevens. Happy Days.

The armament aboard cruisers also received regular attention, and I worked on one particular cruiser, where the breech mechanism was not part of a gun, but part of the cruiser's Catapult Aircraft, which was activated by an explosive charge.

Cruisers equipped with this device, carried one or two small aircraft, designed to land on water, and they were launched into the air by Catapult Aircraft, to carry out spotting and other duties.

On returning to the ship, the aircraft landed on the water, and was lifted back aboard the cruiser, by means of the Catapult Aircraft's own crane.

The breech mechanism was of a simple design, although the horizontally sliding breech block was both large and heavy. The breech block with its firing gear, operated across an explosion chamber, into which a cartridge case was inserted for firing purposes.

At the extreme end of the explosion chamber there was a removable cast iron perforated spreader that spread out the explosive gases that activated the Catapult.

Other than some difficulty in removing the spreader for cleaning and inspections purposes, no problems arose with the mechanism.

A period of several weeks was also spent on other cruisers servicing and modifying their 6 Mk XXIII BL guns, mounted in turrets. The modification, a major and very exacting one, allowed a finer adjustment to be made in the clearance between the threads in the breech opening of the gun and those on the breech screw of the breech mechanism.

Further work, implementing this modification followed, when towards the end of August 1942, I was detailed to proceed to the Middle Dock Shipyard at South Shields, in County Durham, and overhaul and modify the entire Mk XXIII BL, main armament of the 8,000 ton cruiser H.M.S. Kenya. An account of this spell of duty is related in Chapter 5.

But, before we leave Chatham Dockyard and the R Medway for a while, the following Chapter 4 touches on armament work carried out at H.M. Dockyard Sheerness and at the Queenborough Minesweeping Base that were both situated at the mouth of the R Medway on the Isle of Sheppey in Kent.

CHAPTER 4

Armament work at H.M. Dockyard Sheerness and Queenborough Minesweeping Depot

(At various times during World War II)

Sheerness Dockyard (App. 4) was founded at the mouth of the R Medway in 1665. The Dockyard eventually had water basin facilities and a number of dry docks, while among the various workshops there was a Gun Mounting Shop, similar to the one at Chatham, but smaller. The Yard was also joined to the Royal Naval Barracks, known as H.M.S. Wildfire.

The Royal Naval Armament Department did not maintain a staff of gun fitters at Sheerness Dockyard, and any work required there on armaments was carried out by members of the Chatham Gunwharf Afloat Party, from Chatham Dockyard.

This type of work was known as "Out of Port Duty", and started off with an early morning boat journey, of around nine miles, down the R Medway, from Gillingham Pier, near to Chatham Dockyard, to Cornwallis Jetty at Sheerness Dockyard.

On arrival at the Dockyard, work was carried out on guns or other weapons, and this was followed in the late afternoon by a nine mile boat journey back to Gillingham Pier. During my time with the Afloat Party, I made the trip to Sheerness and back many times.

The work was on the smaller types of ships such as frigates, destroyers and submarines, and the work took place in the water basins and dry docks.

The guns dealt with were mainly of 4" calibre, and below, including the 3" QF 20 cwt gun fitted to submarines, while Depth Charge Throwers came in for their share of attention.

In addition to work on the ships, I did routines in the Gun Mounting Shop, where complete gun mountings, with their guns already assembled, were undergoing repair.

As well as getting to know several of the gun mounting fitters fairly well, I recall that Mr Cornish, the man in charge of the workshop, was very helpful, even when I was employed out on the ships, in providing me with a safe storage place for my tools and equipment.

The boats that transported us up and down the river were known as "Trot Boats" and they conveyed Naval and Dockyard personnel to Sheerness and Chatham and to and from Navy vessels laying out in the river, calling at these various ships was known as "Going around the 'Trot' ".

A Trot boat was a small, one funnel vessel, with a crew consisting of the skipper, an able seaman and an engine attendant. The skipper operated from a small bridge that gave him a good all around view of the boat.

The boat was often packed with about twenty passengers down in the hold and another thirty or more standing or sitting shoulder to shoulder on the upper deck, and getting thoroughly wet when it rained.

Most of my trips were to Sheerness, but on occasions my "mate" and I were "dropped off" to go aboard destroyers out in the Trot, and the ships in the Trot would display a flag if they had liberty men or other passengers requiring transport. Two types of flags were displayed: flag "R" if a Trot boat was required for Chatham, and "N" if one was required for Sheerness.

On one or two occasions we were "dropped off" on to "dead ships", with nobody aboard. In which case the skipper of the boat delivering us made arrangements for us to be "picked up" in the afternoon.

Although it was only a river trip of around nine miles each way, during the years that I made the journey, it was not without incident.

Fog was always a cause of anxiety, as the boat slowly picked its way along the river, with all passengers on the upper deck acting as lookouts.

Rough weather, particularly, immediately off Sheerness Dockyard, could be extremely dangerous for small boats, and it was not uncommon under these conditions for the ferry service to be cancelled, in which case we returned to Chatham by train.

On one occasion the boat got stuck on a sandbank, and although the lack of deck space prevented us from using the "theoretical cure", of moving in unison from side to side of the boat, we did, however, jump up and down, to the skipper's timing, without making the slightest bit of difference. Eventually, the rising tide came to our rescue and lifted us off.

A much more serious incident occurred, in which fortunately no-one was injured, but which, never-the-less, left all of us badly shaken, and strangely enough, it took place before we had left the pontoon like structure of Gillingham Pier.

It occurred in the following manner:

It was the custom for the skipper to "trim the boat", in order to ensure it was on an even keel before leaving the Pier, and he did this by directing passengers, as required, to different parts of the upper deck. When he was satisfied with the "trim", he gave a series of toots on the ship's whistle and away we went.

Unfortunately, on this occasion, the "rubbing chock", which was fitted around the sides of the boat in order to protect it from damage when going alongside other vessels, piers etc. was accidentally resting on part of the pontoon section of the Pier and as a result gave a false reading to the "trimming exercise".

Having arrived early that morning, I had managed to obtain a seat down in the hold just to the rear of the steps connecting the hold to the upper deck, and was settling down for a comfortable journey when it happened.

As we got underway, the "rubbing chock" on the boat was no longer supported by the pontoon and the boat gave a sickening lurch followed by an alarming list, which caused a rush by the occupants of the hold towards the upper deck. The best that I could do in the rush was to get my fingers trodden on as I took a grip on the steps and the crowd scrambled past me.

Then, with several disconcerting rolls, the boat partly righted itself and I made my way to the upper deck, where things were a bit chaotic. Some sailors had been thrown on to the pontoon, others were recovering from sprawling on the deck, and many a shaking hand was lighting a cigarette.

After a while order was restored, the skipper "re-trimmed" the boat and the buzz of conversation about the incident gradually got less as we proceeded down the river.

One last story about the Trot boats, but this time, of a humorous nature.

We had travelled down the river several miles with about thirty naval personnel on the upper deck, when the boat's engines stopped and we were left gently bobbing on the tide.

Up from the engine room came the engine attendant, a huge well tattooed ex. stoker in the Royal Navy, who I already knew very well. He immediately saw in me and my tool box a possible solution to his problems and he asked me if I could help, as he thought the propeller shaft bearings had overheated.

So after I had taken a 2 lb hammer out of my tool box, always an impressive start, the ex-Royal Navy stoker and I made our way to the stern of the boat, where he lifted up some deck boards to reveal the cast iron casing of the propeller shaft bearings. The attendant then returned to the engine room.

At this stage, as I set astride of the cast iron casing, and considered whether to unbolt it or not, I simultaneously tapped thoughtfully on the casing, and "hey presto" away went the engine, much to everybody's delight, including my own.

After replacing the deck boards and giving me his thanks, the ex. stoker disappeared below and we continued our cruise down the river.

From then onwards the crew of at least one Trot boat sang my praises and always endeavoured to find me a dry place when it was raining.

Another Royal Naval establishment in the Sheerness area, where I did a small amount of gun work, was the Queenborough Minesweeping Base (App. 4) situated a little further upstream from Sheerness.

Originally named H.M.S. Wildfire II in November 1939, it was renamed St. Tudno in 1941. Throughout the war ships sailed from Queenborough engaged on keeping the Medway and Thames estuaries and their approaches clear of mines laid in some cases by low flying German aircraft. They included various types, such as contact, electric and acoustic mines.

F.19 - H.M. Trawler Malacolite
This trawler was actually based at Queenborough Minesweeping Depot
(Photo: Queenborough Guildhall Museum, Queenborough, Kent)

F.20 - H.M. Trawler Rolls Royce
Another example of a trawler
(Photo: Queenborough Guildhall Museum, Queenborough, Kent)

F.21 - H.M.S. Royal Marine 1944
A larger type of vessel armed with a gun protected by a gun shield
(Photo: Queenborough Guildhall Museum, Queenborough, Kent)

I visited the Queenborough Base several times, travelling in the Depot's van from Chatham, and dealt with 4" QF guns, mounted on strongly built, and powerful, looking trawlers. Photos F.19 and F.20 show examples of trawlers and F.21 a larger type of vessel.

The guns were in good condition, and no major repairs were required, I also discussed the guns with some of the men engaged on this extremely dangerous task.

These were my only visits to Queenborough Minesweeping Base, but at various times throughout the War, I continued to work in Sheerness Dockyard.

CHAPTER 5

**South Shields on the R Tyneand
The cruiser H.M.S. Kenya**

27th August 1942 to 7th December 1942

During August 1942, another spell of detached duty came my way, when I was detailed to proceed to the Middle Dock Shipyard at South Shields in Co Durham and overhaul and modify the twelve 6" BL Mk XXIII guns of the 8,000 ton cruiser H.M.S. Kenya (F.22), a task that lasted for a little over three months.

This was a gun on which I was well experienced and I had performed the modification previously on a number of cruisers at Chatham Dockyard, but never to the extent of twelve guns. Also, owing to the extensive, nature of the job, a "fitter's mate" from the Afloat Party was to accompany me, which was most unusual on detached duty. A middle aged man named Jack Bunyard was selected, I knew him well and he was an excellent assistant.

The tools and special equipment required in aid of the work were sent on in advance. On our own arrival, we found accommodation at Lawe Road in South Shields, where Mr & Mrs McGiffen, a middle aged couple, ran a very congenial boarding house, which in pre-War days, had catered for Music

Hall artists, many of them well known in their day. Wartime regulations however introduced as a result of enemy bombing, forbad people to gather in such places as theatres etc. and had also put an end to Music Hall artists requiring accommodation at South Shields.

F.22 - H.M.S. Kenya was in Middle Dock South Shields in 1942 undergoing repairs to damage caused by enemy action (Photo: Royal Naval Museum, H.M. Naval Base, Portsmouth, Hampshire)

Mrs McGiffen was a rather plump lady with a ready smile and a friendly disposition. Mr McGiffen who was extremely thin, had a good sense of humour, and always vowed that the bed clothes had not touched him for the last ten years. He worked in Middle Dock, and had served in the Merchant Navy. They were both Salvation Army people and had a deep understanding of human nature.

The Middle Dock proved to be a very busy and clean looking shipyard, and on arriving there, I reported to one of the Yard's Officials, and then made my way to the large dry dock, where H.M.S. Kenya lay in the northern sunshine, with her guns dominating the scene. She was a splendid looking ship launched on 18th August 1939 and completed on 28th August 1940. Her armament consisted of twelve 6" Mk XXIII BL guns, eight 4" QF anti-aircraft guns, sixteen smaller guns, six 21" torpedo tubes, and she had a speed of thirty three knots.

Her twelve 6" BL guns were housed in four turrets, with three guns in each turret and in common with all Royal Navy ships, the turrets were designated from forward to aft as "A", "B", "X" and "Y" turrets and it was the custom for the guns of "X" turret to be manned by the Royal Marines.

I walked a short distance around the dockside to the ship's gangway and went aboard H.M.S. Kenya, and making my way to one of the turrets, entered it through a massive steel door, situated in its rear section.

Once inside the turret, I was on familiar territory, in the spacious area behind the guns. The lighting was good and in the roof of the turret, above each gun was a steel eyebolt, to which a chain lifting block could be hung, in order to lift the heavier components of the mechanism.

The manually operated breech mechanism was the latest and probably the final development in manually operated Breech Loading (BL) guns, and its breech mechanism weighed 434 lbs (approx. 196 kg). It embodied several new features that enabled the breech to be opened and closed at a very fast speed. There was also a "misfire stop", an innovation of great importance. It operated in a pendulum like manner and on the breech being closed it locked the breech in the closed position, so that it could not be opened.

On the gun being fired and recoil taking place, the "misfire stop" swung to a position that allowed the breech to be opened. If on the other hand the gun had not recoiled, as would be the case during a misfire, the breech remained locked in the closed position.

One of the misfires that this device guarded against was the "hang fire", in which the cordite charge in the chamber of the gun was smouldering, but did not explode. If the breech was then opened, under the false impression that the gun had fired, the in-rush of air could cause the charge to explode with devastating results.

So, having brought the tools and equipment aboard the work got under way. All the breech mechanisms received similar treatment, namely strip, examine, repair, modify, reassemble and test.

The modification was on the actual gun itself, with the gun in situation in the turret. It entailed very accurate work on the top and bottom lugs that supported the breech mechanism's carrier.

The work involved securing a steel drilling post, with an adjustable arm, to the gun and using a hand operated ratchet for drilling purposes. This was a very sound method that gave you good control during the drilling operation. "Tapping Out" holes to form threads and a degree of filing also took place, and during the ensuing months the work went along steadily.

All went well at our accommodation, which was always a pleasant haven after a day's work. The scene at Mrs McGiffen's house, with its changing group of wartime guests, always reminded me of a play I had seen around 1932. The play centred around the activities of a group of people living in an apartment block.

During our time at Mrs McGiffen's house the guests

included a group of Wrens, several young Royal Marine Officers, a lady visiting her husband, who was serving on H.M.S. Kenya, a young Merchant Navy Officer, who was studying at a local nautical college, a Yorkshire engineer, an Irishman employed at a printing works, two members of my own department who were stationed on the Tyne for the duration of the War, and finally Jack and I, while Mr & Mrs McGiffen presided, unobtrusively over the scene, as their daily help, a young lady popped in and out from the "wings". This completed the setting for a play.

Back aboard H.M.S. Kenya, everything continued to go well, and also, during my time on H.M.S. Kenya, I received departmental instructions to deal with two requests for assistance on naval armaments, that had arisen on the R Tyne.

In response to one of the requests, an Admiralty van took my assistant Jack and I to Palmer's Shipyard, Jarrow-on-Tyne where a section of a catapult aircraft required some attention.

On arriving at Palmer's Yard, we were greeted by a caretaker, who led us to a deserted and apparently closed down area of the Yard, where a section of a catapult was neatly positioned on a shelf like arrangement, out in the open.

Its problem was similar to the one I had worked on in Chatham Dockyard, where the cast iron spreader in the explosion chamber had proved difficult to remove. This one turned out to be much more difficult, and I soon realised that I was on a "hiding to nothing job" with every prospect that I would break the cast iron spreader during my efforts to remove it.

After one or two futile efforts to release it, Jack soaked it in de-rusting fluid, obtained from the caretaker, although I realised it was heat oxidation and not ordinary rust that was holding it.

So, accepting the risk of breaking the spreader, I secured

one end of a rope strop over the "T" piece handle of the spreader and passed one end of a wooden hand spike through the other end of the strop.

Then utilising the side of the catapult as a fulcrum, I gave a series of sharp pulls on the hand spike and the spreader fell with a metallic thud into the explosion chamber, and after cleaning and lightly greasing the spreader and its seating, it was time to say cheerio to the caretaker and return to South Shields.

The other problem found us travelling by Admiralty van to a berth on the R Tyne, where a trawler had reported that they could not open the breech of their 4" QF gun. As we travelled along, I reflected on possible causes of this, such as a broken horn on the crank that opened and closed the breech.

Once aboard, I reported to the skipper and then I made my way to the gun, which was mounted near the bow of the trawler. Very soon I was surrounded by a group of crew members, all keen to watch my introduction to the gun.

At this stage two members of the crew removed the canvass covers at the rear of the gun shield and all was revealed.

The breech mechanism was covered by a mixture of rust and salt sea spray which had sealed the breech block solid. This was the result of heavy and dangerous seas sweeping over the ship's bow to penetrate the steel gun shield and its canvass covers and to corrode the breech mechanism. I reserved my judgement as to the cause, as it could still be a broken component.

The first thing was to remove some of the rust mixture, so after a liberal washing down with paraffin and some careful scraping to remove the rust etc. all was ready for the first attempt to open the breech.

Despite much pulling on the breech mechanism lever, the

breech block refused to move. Gradually as all else failed, my efforts became less scientific and finally, while I pulled on the breech mechanism lever, and my assistant Jack thumped away on the other end of the breech block with a small baulk of timber, the breech block slowly gave up its resistance, and in a series of short jerks moved to the open position.

I stripped the mechanism down, without too much trouble, everything was cleaned, examined, lightly greased, reassembled, and having checked the mechanism for correct function, I reported to the skipper that the gun's breech mechanism was in a serviceable condition.

The last I saw of the gun, as I left the ship, was two members of the crew busily engaged in replacing the canvass covers.

Aboard H.M.S. Kenya, I was extremely pleased with things, and with the turrets mostly to ourselves the work progressed in an excellent manner. As each turret was completed the weeks gradually amounted to months and by the beginning of December 1942 the job was completed.

Then having arranged for the tools and equipment to be returned to Chatham Gunwharf, it was time to say cheerio to a number of the staff at Middle Dock and to thank Mr & Mrs McGiffen for their welcome and kind hospitality, for which the "Geordies" are so well known.

So like a couple of "homing pigeons" Jack and I caught the train back to Chatham, with a change of trains at London.

CHAPTER 6

Armament Work in H.M. Dockyard Chatham
12th December 1942 to 17th July 1943

On returning from South Shields, I reported back to H.M. Gunwharf Chatham and after a few days leave I rejoined the Afloat Party in Chatham Dockyard, for what proved to be a seven month or so period of work.

The armaments worked on, in this, and other periods of work in the Dockyard, included Sub-Calibre guns, Automatic guns, Holman Projectors etc.

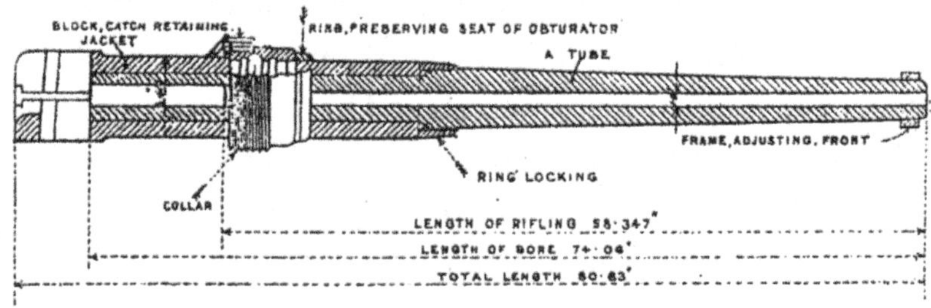

F.23 - A Hotchkiss 3 Pdr QF Sub-Calibre Gun

The Sub-Calibre gun (F.23) was used for practice purposes only, and in a somewhat unusual manner. It was in fact inserted and secured into the breech end of a larger calibre gun (F.24). The larger gun was then put through its drill routines, but only the Sub-Calibre gun with its smaller ammunition was loaded and fired.

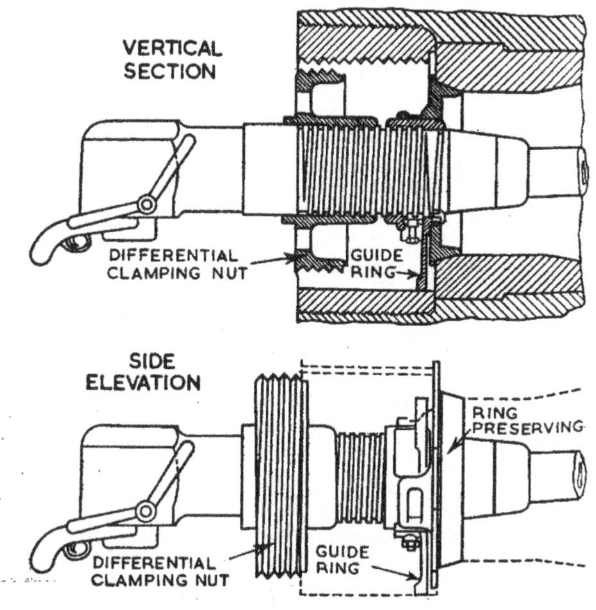

F.24 - A Hotchkiss QF Sub-Calibre Gun assembled to a larger gun for practice firing

This conserved the larger guns' shells and cordite charges, and curtailed wear on the larger guns' rifling. Comparisons were also made between the results of the "Sub-Calibre Shoot" and the probable results if the larger gun had been fired.

A certain terminology was associated with Sub-Calibre guns. The larger gun was known as the "parent" gun, while "shipping the Sub-Calibre" referred to assembling it to the "parent" gun, and trial in place was the process of ensuring that the Sub-Calibre gun operated correctly when assembled to the "parent" gun.

There were three main types of Sub-Calibre guns, the standard 6 Pdr and 3 Pdr QF Hotchkiss guns which were modified for this purpose by means of several alterations, including the addition of a "screwed collar" that secured it to the "parent" Breech Loading gun.

The third type was a 2 Pdr QF Sub-Calibre gun used on QF guns.

The 6 Pdr Hotchkiss gun with its mechanism weighed 849 lb (385 kg) and was used in conjunction with 15" BL guns, and the 3 Pdr Hotchkiss gun with its mechanism weighed 528lb (239 kg) and was used extensively on 6" Mk XXIII BL guns in turrets. Extreme care was required when working on these guns, if accidents were to be avoided, especially in the confined space of 8" BL gun turrets.

I only worked on a 6 Pdr Sub-Calibre once but fitted and conducted "trials in place" on around twenty five 3 Pdr Sub-Calibre guns, aboard such cruisers as H.M.S. Sheffield, Southampton, and Belfast. These ships had a main armament of twelve

6" BL Mk XXIII guns, "housed" in four turrets, with three guns in each turret and every one of these 6" guns had its own 3 Pdr Hotchkiss QF Sub-Calibre gun, "stowed" inside the turret, close to its "parent" gun.

The 2 Pdr Sub-Calibre gun was specially designed for Sub-Calibre work and was very much smaller and lighter than the 3 Pdr Hotchkiss. It was used on QF guns, assembled to the "parent" gun from the breech end, in the usual manner, but was secured in position by being screwed to the breech face of the gun.

One ship in particular that I recall working on was the Polish Navy's cruiser "Dragon" on which I spent several days fitting 2 Pdr Sub-Calibre guns to her 4" QF guns. During which time I was ably assisted by a group of Polish sailors, who manhandled the Sub-

Calibres from their stowages down below deck to the various gun decks, where the 4" QF guns were mounted in open gun shields.

Other types of guns which received attention on a regular basis were the Royal Navy's QF automatic guns, which rapidly increased in numbers during World War II.

F.25 - A bank of four 2 Pdr Mk VIII QF Guns
(Photo: Explosion Museum of Naval Firepower, Priddy's Hard, Gosport, Hampshire)

They consisted of five main types, as follows, together with the appropriate dates they came into service, shown in brackets.

The Vickers 2 Pdr QF Mk II Pom-Pom (1915), Vickers 2 Pdr QF Mk VIII (1930), Vickers 0.5 QF machine gun (1932), the Swiss 20mm QF Oerlikon (1939) and the Swedish 40mm QF Bofors gun (1941).

The Vickers 2 Pdr Mk II was used in the Fleet during World

War I (1914-1918), but in World War II, it was employed mainly on Royal Navy Auxiliary vessels.

The Vickers 2 Pdr Mk II was the forerunner of the Vickers 2 Pdr Mk VIII that gave widespread service in World War II.

The 2 Pdr Mk VIII (F.25) was a recoil operated gun with a water cooled barrel, and its ammunition was contained in steel "articulating links" that could be "hooked" together to form a belt.

Admiralty records show that 6,691 2 Pdr Mk VIII guns were made in Britain.

Those that I worked on were in either four gun or single gun mountings. The gun was extremely good to work on, owing to the excellent design of the mechanism, with its ready access for stripping, assembling and testing purposes.

A single 2 Pdr VIII gun, known as a "bow chaser" was sometimes mounted close to the bow of destroyers, in order to better engage German "E" boats at close quarters.

An interesting feature of the 2 Pdr Mk VIII gun, was a rounds counter that recorded, and showed on a dial the number of rounds that had been fired.

The 2 Pdr Mk VIII had a range of 6,800 yards (6220m) 3.86 miles.

The firm of Vickers Ltd also produced the 0.5 calibre, recoil operated water cooled machine gun, with its ammunition of solid bullets, contained in link fed belts.

The guns were in quadruple mountings, with the four guns mounted one above the other, and staggered in the horizontal plane.

They were used, as well as for other purposes, against attacks by low flying aircraft at close quarters.

Another automatic gun introduced into the Royal Naval service was the Oerlikon 20mm, air cooled, magazine fed gun. The Oerlikon was mostly mounted, as a single gun, in a free swinging mounting, in which the gun was trained and elevated by one operator, using the shoulder pieces attached to the gun.

It had a range of 4,800 yards (4389m) 2.92 miles.

They were widely distributed throughout the Fleet and some battleships included 20 or more Oerlikon guns in their anti-aircraft armament.

F.26 - A Single Bofors Gun, with an air cooled barrel

Many ships included in their armament the 40mm Bofors, a recoil operated gun, mounted in single and twin gun mountings. The barrel of the single gun (F.26) was air cooled and those of the twin mounting (F.27) cooled by water circulated around each gun by a pump.

The gun was suitable for both air and surface firing and had a range of 10,730 yards (9,832m) 6.1 miles.

F.27 - Twin 40mm QF Bofors Guns, fitted with water cooled barrels
(Official Photo)

I worked on many Bofors guns, including the single mountings but mostly on the twins. It was not exactly my favourite gun to work on, with its heavy automatic loader, which had to be manhandled, out and in, during the stripping and reassembling operations, while the breech mechanism, with its breech closing spring, was not easily accessible.

F.28 - The Holman Projector

As regards the smaller calibre machine guns, such as the Lewis, Bren, Lancaster, Hotchkiss etc. they were repaired and tested at H.M. Gunwharf, Chatham.

A rather unusual weapon, used by the Royal Navy, against low flying aircraft, was a mortar type bomb thrower, known as the Holman Projector, and its care and maintenance came under the Royal Naval Armament Department.

It was developed and manufactured, by Holman Brothers Ltd, at Camborne in Cornwall, and I worked on the Mk II model, of which 2,500 were made.

The Mk II model (F.28) consisted of an upright steel tube with a small cylindrical compressed air container secured to its base. A valve controlled by a trigger mechanism, operated by a member of the crew, could be opened to allow the compressed air to blow a mills grenade out of the projector.

The compressed air was supplied from a series of high pressure air bottles installed aboard the ship.

A light metal canister, open at one end, into which the grenade fitted, provided the safety device that ensured the grenade was at a safe distance from the ship before it exploded. The explosion also created a large cloud of black smoke that interfered with accurate bombing and machine gunning.

Holman Projectors were fitted to many ships, such as destroyers, motor launches and trawlers and some of the successes achieved with the aid of Holman Projectors are shown in (App. 7).

In Chatham Dockyard there were many large workshops and among them was the Gun Mounting Shop. It was a large, high roofed building, with plenty of floor space on which a variety of complete gun mountings were accommodated, as fitters and others used their expertise, to bring the mountings, with their intricate firing gear, and recoil and recuperating systems back to first class condition.

I worked in the Gun Mounting Shop on many occasions, and always received a congenial and often jocular welcome from members of the staff when I arrived to fit breech mechanisms to those guns that had been assembled to their mountings.

The Gun Mounting Shop also had its own Afloat Party, who in addition to overhauling gun mountings aboard ships, also applied their extensive knowledge and engineering skills to maintaining the machinery of 8" and 6" etc. gun turrets. I also enjoyed a good relationship with the members of this Party, who I met on a regular basis as I moved from ship to ship.

My activities in Chatham Dockyard were curtailed for a while in July 1943, when I was detailed to report for duty at the Admiralty Shore Establishment at Lyness, on the Isle of Hoy, Orkney, for a six months spell of duty, and Chapter 7 that follows, gives a glimpse of that period and of the Home Fleet as it lay at anchor in the great Harbour of Scapa Flow.

CHAPTER 7

With the Home Fleet at Scapa Flow, Orkney
18th July 1943 to 15th January 1944

Another spell of detached duty came my way in mid 1943, this time at the vast Naval base of Scapa Flow in Orkney. It entailed servicing the guns of the Home Fleet and those of Commonwealth Navies.

Scapa Flow was a high security area and before travelling I was issued with a special pass, showing my photograph and other details.

Then having arranged for my ever faithful tool box to be sent on in advance, I was ready to depart from Chatham, on the 18th July 1943: destination, the Admiralty Establishment, Lyness, Isle of Hoy, Orkney.

My wife Joyce, with our eighteen month old son Richard, travelled up to London with me, to give me a good send off. A special "Orkney and Northern Scotland" train, the "Jellicoe", was standing at the London station's departure platform when we arrived. It was due to make only two stops between London and Thurso in the North of Scotland, where from nearby Scrabster, a boat would complete the final stage of the journey, across the Pentland Firth to Orkney.

The station platform was packed with uniformed members of the three services, both male and female, with a sprinkling of allied personnel in uniforms and a few civilians.

Hundreds of farewells were taking place as mothers, wives, sweethearts, relations and friends kissed, embraced and shook hands as they took their fond farewells, as the train prepared to leave.

My wife, my son, and I took our own fond farewells, and I climbed aboard the train, which was soon chugging its way out of the station, while as many heads as possible protruded out of the carriage windows to return the waves of the crowded throng on the station platform, who certainly gave us a good send off.

The corridor type carriage of the train was absolutely full with uniformed figures, standing, and before long, sitting in the corridor. I managed to get a seat which during the course of the journey I vacated several times, on a "lease lend" basis, in order to let some of the sufferers in the corridor have a sit down.

As the "Jellicoe" showed its paces and sped northwards, we passed the time away with spells of conversation and longer spells of fitful sleeping, until at last we crossed the Scottish border, and eventually stopped the other side of Motherwell Station, where members of the Salvation Army greeted us with their traditional good will and large cups of tea. A Cockney type humorist had evidently preceded us through Motherwell station, for inscribed in chalk beneath the Motherwell sign, were the words "Father Well too".

Following the welcome break for refreshments we all settled down again as the train sped on its way across Scotland, to arrive at the small port of Thurso, in Northern Scotland, where we left the train. A number of motor coaches then conveyed us to the nearby harbour of Scrabster, where a boat was waiting to take us to Orkney.

At Scrabster, heightened security measures became apparent, for a barbed wire enclosure surrounded the embarkation area, and Royal Navy ratings, with fixed bayonets, were on guard.

After a careful inspection of my pass, I was allowed to board the boat, to take up a sheltered position on the upper deck.

The crossing of the Pentland Firth could best be described as "fair, with a tendency to get worse", and as such claimed its quota of seasick passengers. On arriving at Lyness the boat tied up alongside the "Dunluce Castle", an ex. Union Castle liner, acting as the waterfront "gateway" to Lyness.

All civilians arriving at Lyness had to pass through a security office, aboard the "Dunluce Castle" to be identified.

At Lyness the Admiralty had established a "minor" Dockyard with among other facilities, a large stone quay, storehouses, workshops, a foundry, a floating dock out in the flow, and my destination, the Royal Naval Armament Department's Gun Repair Workshop.

On higher land, to the rear of the "Dockyard", there was an area with large wooden huts built on it. These huts provided the living quarters for the large number of Admiralty and private firm employees that had arrived on the Isle of Hoy.

Each hut contained about sixteen cubicles, and one of these became my accommodation when I was ashore.

It proved to be an unforgettable six months, spent out in the Flow, working on the guns of battleships, cruisers, destroyers and other vessels, and conversing with a wide range of naval personnel including "hostilities only" entries (F.32), enlisted for the duration of the War. It was indeed a great privilege of which I was always fully appreciative.

After getting settled into my cubicle, I reported to the Gun Repair Workshop, in the Dockyard area. It was a strongly constructed building and contained an engineering workshop and a joinery section. The staff numbered about twenty three men, most of them on "detached duty" from Armament Depots throughout the United Kingdom, and of this number, six fitters and six "fitter's' mates", worked on a regular basis out in the Flow.

I spent a couple of days in the gunnery workshop, overhauling a 2 Pdr Mk VIII Pom-Pom and then moved out into the Flow to initially, carry out standard routines on the 4" Mk XVI, QF twin mounted guns, of several destroyers.

This type of gun occupied my attention many times, and often involved modifying the gun's striker cocking system, as I had done in Chatham Dockyard, and once again my "own made" hacksaw, designed for working in restricted places, did excellent work, and was often loaned to other fitters.

Shortly after this, I received my first emergency "call out". It came from a cruiser, that had managed to jam a 6 Pdr Hotchkiss Sub-Calibre gun, in the breech opening of one of the cruisers 8" calibre turret guns.

At first sight it looked a very sorry business, with the Sub-Calibre gun tilted at a steep angle and its breech end suspended from the roof of the turret by means of slings and lifting gear. Its muzzle was hidden from view, inside the breech end of the 8" gun.

The situation was one in which a false move could have resulted in serious damage to both guns, especially to the 8" gun's "cone seating" which helped to seal the explosive gases when the 8" gun was fired.

However, after removing any components that were likely to obstruct the extraction of the gun, and assisted by members of the turret gun's crew in adjusting the position of the 8" gun as required, the Sub-Calibre gun was eventually retrieved from its precarious position.

So, after reporting back to the Gunnery Officer and saying thank you and cheerio to members of the Gunnery Section, I headed back in the Armament Departments boat to Lyness.

After I had been at the Lyness Depot for about a month, one of the island's policemen came to my cubicle to inform me that I had been transferred from my previous Home Guard Unit of the Royal West Kent Regiment at Chatham, Kent, to the 2nd Battalion of the Orkney Home Guard Unit, of the Seaforth Highlanders Regiment.

I duly reported to the Unit's Lyness Headquarters, to be issued with a new uniform, and after this I attended as many parades as my work in the Flow allowed.

The unit had its own piper and a Regular Army Instructor, from the King's Own Borderers, whose sole purpose in life seemed to centre around ordering us to fix bayonets and charge at a large grass covered bank he had discovered in the vicinity.

So, to the skirl of the pipes, we headed for bayonet practice, on a regular basis.

During these sessions, he came near to unnerving us, as in a rich Scottish dialect, he repeatedly exalted us to "Charge and Let Them Have It".

Also, around this time I obtained permission to use part of our community cinema for physical culture classes. However, owing to the complete lack of volunteers the classes never materialised.

But, nevertheless, for the rest of my time at Lyness, I continued to use the cinema facility at least once a week for training sessions.

During the months that followed I worked on numerous ships, but only a few are mentioned in this chapter, and these ships serve to show the type of work carried out.

On occasions, I lived aboard a ship for several days or so at a time, a process known as being "victualled aboard". This included living in a Mess, receiving a daily "tot" of rum and drawing your hammock.

An ex. fishing boat, on loan to the Armament Department, transported us on a regular basis between Lyness Jetty and the ships.

All the ships' Mess Decks, whose hospitality I enjoyed during World War II, had one thing in common. It was the deadly silence that came over the Mess when Sir Winston Churchill broadcast one of his famous speeches over the radio. Anyone breaking the silence was quickly rebuked in "basic English" by a vocal chorus from the rest of the Mess.

A rather unusual job occurred late one evening, aboard a 6" gun cruiser. One of its 6" BL turret guns had a copper deposit blocking a section of its rifling.

Copper deposits of this nature, came from the raised copper driving band that encircled the lower part of the shell. When the shell was rammed home, the copper driving band "bit" into the rifling of the gun and on the gun being fired, and as the shell travelled up the bore of the gun, the twist in the rifling of the gun, imparted a twist to the shell, about its longitudinal axis. This twist on the shell improved its range and accuracy.

Fortunately, in this case, the deposit in the rifling was near to the breech end of the gun, although it was still difficult to remove as the heat developed during firing, made the copper extremely hard.

The work entailed using a scraper like tool attached to a long steel rod, to scrape steadily away at the deposit, while the interior of the bore of the gun was lit up by means of an electric light on a "wandering lead".

Working in these cramped conditions placed a strain on the neck and the back and required another fitter and myself, taking it in turns at the scraping. After working well into the night our efforts were rewarded and the deposit was removed.

Another cruiser that I worked on was H.M.A.S. Shropshire, transferred from the Royal Navy to the Royal Australian Navy in 1942, to replace H.M.A.S. Canberra, lost in action against the Japanese Navy at the Battle of Sava Island, in the Pacific during 8th - 9th August 1942.

H.M.A.S. Shropshire's armament consisted of eight 8" BL guns, in twin turrets, eight 4" Mk XVI QF guns in twin mountings and eighteen smaller guns.

The 4" QF guns were the focus of my attention and my terms of reference were to strip, examine and reassemble H.M.A.S. Shropshire's complete armament of 4" QF guns.

Once aboard, I contacted the Chief Ordnance Artificer and obtained his permission to use the ship's Ordnance Workshop.

The weather kept fine and the work on the guns went along steadily, and while I was aboard, I noted the Australians' great pleasure in physical culture activities as in the evenings they gathered on the upper deck, to engage in such activities as exercises, skipping, boxing and weight lifting.

During my conversations with them, swimming was a very popular topic, and some of them had represented their clubs, or areas, in Australian swimming events. I am also very pleased to say that during one of my off duty periods I was able to join them in one of their physical culture sessions.

Work on the guns continued to go well, and with no major problems arising, progressed to a successful conclusion, and it was time to leave H.M.A.S. Shropshire. Then having said cheerio to the Chief Ordnance Artificer and his staff, and wished them well for the future, I boarded my boat back to Lyness to spend the evening in my cubicle, catching up on my letter writing.

After this a number of destroyers with their 2 Pdr Mk VIII QF guns, kept me busy, followed by a spell on the 11,553 ton, cruiser H.M.S. Belfast (F.29) which was launched on the 17th March 1938 and commissioned on the 5th August 1939.

F.29 - H.M.S. Belfast, one of the cruisers that took part in the Battle of North Cape, off Norway, on the26th December 1943 (Photograph: I.W.M, HU4646, Copyright Imperial War Museum)

She had the impressive armament of twelve 6" Mk XXIII BL guns, mounted in triple gun turrets, twelve 4" Mk XVI QF guns in twin mountings and a number of smaller guns.

My work lay in the spacious 6" gun turrets, servicing the breech mechanisms and fitting 3 Pdr Hotchkiss Sub-Calibre guns to the 6" guns. Each gun had its own 3 Pdr Sub-Calibre gun which was stored inside the turret, in close proximity to its own 6" gun.

I was "victualled aboard" H.M.S. Belfast and the work in the turrets went extremely well and in keeping with H.M.S. Belfast's state of readiness, the breech mechanisms of the 6" guns were always left fully assembled at the end of each day's work.

One evening, a little later however, my activities on the guns of H.M.S. Belfast suddenly ceased, when a strident call came over the ship's loud speakers, and it was to the effect that "all civilian workmen aboard are to muster on the upper deck immediately ready to go ashore, as the ship is going to sea".

From that moment onwards it was all go, as I quickly gathered my possessions and assembled on the upper deck, in company with several Dockyard workmen, also bent on going ashore.

After a short wait we were transferred to a hastily summoned fishing boat and returned as ever to Lyness.

On the morning of Friday 13th August 1943 I was out in the Flow engaged on a bank of four 40mm Bofors guns, aboard one of the following capital ships "Renown" "Malaya" or "Anson".

Sometime during the morning, and completely out of the blue, it was announced over the ship's loud speakers, that His Majesty King George VI would be visiting the ship, and members of the ship's company would parade on the upper deck for His Majesty's inspection.

About twenty minutes later, a further announcement was made to the effect, that any civilian workmen aboard, who would like to parade along with the ship's company, should hand their names in at the ship's office. I immediately hurried to the ship's office and recorded my name.

Then, after I had cooled down a bit, I reflected that my attire of greasy overalls, white "Fearnought" jacket, thick roll neck sweater and calf length leather boots, did not seem to fit the occasion and I considered withdrawing my name.

I expressed my doubts to a midshipman, who was standing nearby and he promptly suggested that perhaps he and his fellow midshipmen may be able to help, an offer that after a little hesitation I accepted.

The midshipman thereupon mustered a number of his fellow midshipmen, and between them, they fitted me out with a brand new outfit.

First, after trying on several pairs of shoes, one of the midshipmen, came up with a pair that fitted me. Another one supplied a shirt and tie, I think it was an Eton tie, while a pair of grey flannel trousers, a superbly fitting brown sports jacket, and a pair of socks were contributed by other midshipmen.

The transformation was very satisfying and I paraded on the upper deck in the front rank along with members of the ship's company and several Dockyard men.

His Majesty King George VI dressed in Naval uniform, proceeded to inspect the front rank and although His Majesty stopped in front of me, His Majesty moved on a little and spoke to the Dockyard man standing on my immediate right hand side, enquiring how long the man had been in the Flow, and what was his home base. To which the man replied, stating a period of time, and giving his home base as Plymouth.

Then after wishing the man an early return to his family at Plymouth, His Majesty carried on down the line to complete his inspection.

This particular visit of His Majesty King George VI to Scapa Flow, lasted from Thursday 12th August to Sunday 15th August and included visits to some ships of the Home Fleet and to those of other Navies and to a number of places ashore (App. 1 refers). A total of twelve ships were programmed to be inspected, including one submarine.

Although the August weather at this time was quite sunny and bright, there was a warning chill in the air, with rain never far away. There were times, however, when sunshine and atmospheric conditions, combined to give the Flow and its surrounding islands, an enchanted appearance, where every feature stood out crystal clear.

But generally speaking the winter weather during my time in the Flow was certainly bad, with spells of rain, accompanied by strong winds, and snow blizzards that restricted the vision to three or four feet. The blizzards came up without warning and ceased just as suddenly.

The fact that small haystacks in the Lyness area were only prevented from being blown away by means of throwing a stout rope net over them and securing the net to the ground with metal spikes, shows the force of the wind.

As regards the Flow itself, it could be really rough, and at other times, so smooth that you could see the ripples on its surface as shoals of fish swam across the Flow.

Another interesting feature of the Flow, were the seals which could be seen basking on the surrounding rocks. One particular solitary seal seemed to have formed a liking for the ship, the Dunluce Castle at Lyness.

It was a regular visitor and could be seen near the ship, with its head just above the water as it studied the ship and the Lyness landscape.

In relation to warm clothing to help combat the winter weather, it was the custom in our Southern Armament Depots to issue each member of the Afloat Party with a very warm white "Fearnought" jacket.

But, in this respect the Scapa Flow Afloat Party surpassed all with the issue of a Fearnought jacket, long oilskin coat with a south-wester hat, knee length white woolly socks and calf length leather or rubber boots. It was indeed a most necessary attire.

A fascinating phenomenon in Orkney is the "Midnight Sun" which I was fortunate to see. It occurred around mid summer, and for several weeks there was very little darkness. The light appeared to me, to be similar to very pale green neon lighting and in order to check its brilliance I stood by the window of my cubicle and read a few paragraphs of a newspaper by means of its midnight light.

I continued to attend Home Guard parades, but with a change of duties, that entailed taking care of the Unit's weapons and ensuring they were correctly stored and maintained.

The Lyness Home Guard Unit also added a voluntary unarmed combat class to its activities, it was aimed at the younger members of the Unit, among which, at the age of thirty years, I placed myself.

A regular Army Instructor arrived to take the first session, held in a small wooden hut, with about a dozen of us in attendance.

After introducing himself the instructor explained a series of unarmed combat moves, including how to use a "tin hat" as an offensive weapon.

At this stage, he called for a volunteer, to assist with the demonstrations and being fairly fit from my regular training, and in order to help the class along, I offered my services.

My first contribution was to stand out in front of the class, acting as a model, while he pointed out the vulnerable parts of the body. Then, as if by magic, he produced a set of boxing gloves, which certainly had not figured in my calculations, and declared that he would now demonstrate on me some of the more important blows to be considered. I was not too perturbed at this, as from the age of 15 to about 18 I had also belonged to the boxing club run by Shorts Bros, the aircraft engineers at Rochester in Kent.

Prior to commencing, he emphasised that you should never "pull your punches" in practice, as otherwise you tended to do it when it was for real, he also added "always be on your guard".

Having donned our gloves, he announced that sparring would commence, during the course of which he would further demonstrate the punches already referred to. This was followed by a stinging blow to my head, which he explained to the class, served to illustrate the need to always be on your guard.

We sparred and demonstrated the selected punches for about ten minutes during which time I managed to keep out of trouble, although I had the feeling that the proceedings had outgrown the demonstration stage.

After he had answered one or two questions from the class, he said he would now show how the various throws and holds that he had demonstrated could be used in actual combat.

This was my signal to speak up and I told him that I had wrestled professionally and had no wish to inflict or receive unnecessary injuries in a no punches pulled demonstration.

It was of no avail, and he came at me like a tornado, and I was soon thankful for all those years spent in training and practicing the art of wrestling and learning judo throws and locks without ever wearing the traditional white jacket etc.

Very soon the small hut was creaking and shaking as we struggled, still on our feet, seeking the opening for a throw, while the other members of the class stood well back clear of the action.

The hut was still creaking and shaking four minutes or so later, as I continued to resist his onslaught, I was used to savage attacks by some wrestlers, and knew that if you could keep out of trouble, they usually and hopefully tired first.

There was no sign of this, as he was obviously very fit but anticipating his grasp as he advanced towards me, I threw him with my favourite throw, the cross buttock.

The cross-buttock was a devastating throw, in which the main weight of the thrower's body falls on his opponent, who is underneath as they hit the floor together.

Once the instructor and I hit the floor, the ground wrestling, with its great variety of locks and throws commenced, and after a brief struggle, I succeeded in pinning him to the floor, with a "scissors" on one of his arms, my body laying across his chest and an arm lock on the other arm.

We regained our feet, and with very little respite, started again, with as much fervour as before.

It only went on for a few minutes as evading his attempt at a head lock, I threw him again with another cross buttock, followed up by a "pin fall" in which after straddling his body, as he lay flat on the floor, I pinned his arms and legs above his head, and it was all over, thank goodness.

The evening was both the beginning and the ending of the unarmed combat class, I was sorry, but certainly not surprised.

I never saw the instructor or any members of the class again, and resumed my more sedate activities of looking after the armoury although I continued with my personal training programme.

I also managed to watch some excellent football matches played on the pitches at Lyness. The teams came from the battleships, cruisers, destroyers etc. anchored out in the Flow.

A number of professional footballers, who had been "called up" for war service, took part in the games in which members of the ships' companies including many high ranking officers, lined the touch line to give their vocal support.

Work out in the Flow continued to occupy my attention, with only rare periods ashore, working in the Department's workshop.

On one occasion, following a signal from the 16" gun battleship H.M.S. Nelson, I found myself aboard the Depot's boat headed towards H.M.S. Nelson, to deal with a problem the nature of which I had not been informed.

The boat landed me safely aboard H.M.S. Nelson and then took off immediately on another mission. I reported to the Gunnery Officer who informed me that the problem had now been sorted out, and no help was required.

So I spent a restful three hours or so, sitting in the sunshine and using the outside of a 16" Gun Turret as a back rest, until the boat returned to pick me up.

Another battleship I worked on provided a most unusual experience. While I was working on one of the ship's anti-aircraft guns, the order came over the ship's loud speakers, that all civilians' work aboard the ship was to stop as a special exercise was about to start.

Safety lines were run out on the upper deck including a number across the ship's beam. Then the exercise commenced, as very slowly the gigantic ship began to take on a list.

This went on for around an hour, until the list reached alarming proportions and the use of the safety lines became very necessary.

The list remained static for a half an hour and then extremely slowly the ship gradually returned to an even heel, and the exercise was over. I never knew the reason for the exercise or by what means it was achieved and I never asked any questions.

The pressure of work did not allow much time to visit places in the area, but I did manage to make one trip to the town of Kirkwall, situated on the Isle of Pomona, known to the Orkney Islanders as the Mainland.

The trip entailed a boat ride across the Flow, from Lyness to Scapa Pier on Pomona, a one way journey of about 14 miles followed by a short bus ride to Kirkwall.

A regular boat service for which no charge was made ran from Lyness and among the passengers on the day that I travelled were a group of housewives, with their shopping baskets, off for a day's shopping in Kirkwall.

On the way across I fell into conversation with a United States naval steward, who was on his way to Kirkwall, to make some catering arrangements for his unit.

The weather remained fine, the sea calm and on arrival I enjoyed a stroll around Kirkwall as I reflected on the town's long association with the affairs of the sea.

I then moved on to have a look at Kirkwall's St Magnus Cathedral, founded in 1139 and Britain's most northerly cathedral.

Built of a red sandstone like material, its appearance was much different from the grey stone of most of our southern cathedrals.

Finally a relaxing trip back to Lyness on the boat brought a very pleasant day to a close.

Towards the latter part of 1943, I was detailed to assist in an investigation aboard a cruiser that had experienced a number of misfires among the guns of her main armament of eight 5.25" QF guns, mounted in twin turrets.

During this time the cruiser was engaged on "working up" trials, aimed at improving her fighting efficiency and highlighting any problems requiring attention.

Misfires with their element of danger, were always a matter of grave concern and it was very important to locate the cause and prevent its reoccurrence.

The depot boat took me out to the cruiser, and on arriving aboard, the Naval Commander in charge of the investigation, greeted me and explained the background to the misfires.

The misfires concerned three of the guns, in which the rounds had misfired at the first time of firing, but had fired at the second or third attempt. The ship's staff had already tested the ship's firing circuits and found them working correctly.

So with the Commander in close attendance I went to work on the breech mechanisms of the three guns firing locks and checked their electric firing needles and found everything in good condition

In addition to these tests, the Commander introduced another piece of test equipment consisting of a twelve inches or so long "sawn off" section of the base of a 5.25" brass cartridge case.

The primer in the base of the case had been removed and replaced by an electric light socket and bulb, specially fitted inside the case.

The test involved loading the case to the gun, closing the breech and bringing the electric firing needle into contact with the light socket, and if all was well the bulb lit up when the current was made and went out when it was switched off. The effects on the bulb were observed by looking down the bore of the gun, from the muzzle end, and all three guns passed the test successfully.

These activities took us from three to four hours, at which stage the Commander gave the breech mechanisms, and their electrical components, the all clear.

The Commander then decided that we would go below, into the ship's magazine and examine samples of the detonators of live cartridge cases.

We entered the magazine and visually examined samples from two batches of cases and found them in order. We then turned our attention to a third batch and soon found a possible cause of the misfires.

For there, spread over the surface of the detonator in the base of one of the cases, was a brownish paste-like substance, that could act as insulation against the electric firing needle, although laboratory tests would be required to establish the nature of the "paste" and its possible source of origin. Quite a number of the detonators in this batch were found to be contaminated in this manner, and the thickness of the deposit varied.

We discussed our findings and concluded as follows. The cartridge case failed to fire at the first attempt, owing to the firing needle being insulated by the "paste". It fired on the second or third attempt as by that time the firing needle had "pierced" or "dispersed" the insulating "paste". The number of attempts could possibly vary in accordance with the thickness of the "paste".

So, after a very interesting day, I said cheerio to the Commander and headed back to base.

Another cruiser on which I spent some time was the Royal New Zealand Navy's cruiser Gambia, which was stationed in the Flow from late October to November 1943, and attached to the 1st Cruiser Squadron for "working up" exercises.

She was commissioned into the Royal New Zealand Navy after being transferred from the Royal Navy, as a replacement for the Royal New Zealand Navy's cruiser Leander, which had been badly damaged during the Solomon Islands Campaign of 1943.

H.M.S. Gambia had a modern armament of twelve 6" Mk XXIII BL Guns, mounted in four turrets, with three guns in each turret, eight 4" Mk XVI QF anti-aircraft guns in twin mountings and sixteen smaller guns.

It was the 4" Mk XVI QF guns that occupied my attention over the next week or so, and during this time I was made very welcome in the Mess and gathered from the general conversation that an election was taking place in New Zealand and the ship's company had received their voting papers.

Work on the guns went very smoothly as I carried out the usual routines and final pass out tests. So it was cheerio to the ship's Ordnance Staff, and on to my next assignment.

While constantly on the move from ship to ship, I was greatly impressed with the talents and skills that I found among the members of ships' companies and civilians working aboard.

This occurred, in the main, when I was sleeping aboard ships, and during my off duty time had the opportunity to meet and talk to people from all walks of life and occupations drawn together in the turmoil of war.

On one occasion I was taking a stroll below deck, on a battleship, when on my way I spoke to an artificer who was carving a Royal Navy ship's crest out of a solid block of wood.

The crest was about eighteen inches high, and he informed me that he had carved several such crests for different ships. He went on to explain that although he was enlisted into the Royal Navy as a carpenter, he was in fact a "carver of angels".

At this stage, I thought, "Hello, here comes the leg pulling", but he went on to tell me that in "civvy street" he was employed in visiting cathedrals, churches etc. in order to repair or carve new angels or other religious figures. As for example if a figure had a broken part such as a wing or a head, he would carve a new one and fit it to the existing figure.

I told him that I was amazed at the way he carved the various features of the crest, but to him it seemed the most natural thing in the world. Such is the artist.

Another, quite different incident occurred, when a group of us were on the upper deck of a cruiser, awaiting the arrival of our boat.

Nearby, a naval rating was doing his best, without any success, to start the engine of one of the ship's large motor boats. The engine showed some promise by spluttering but refused to start.

A civilian in our group became interested and having obtained a "dead match" from a member of our party, asked the rating if he could "have a go".

Having obtained the rating's approval, he bent over the engine and inserted the match into a "vital place" and to everybody's delight, away went the engine.

As we sped towards the shore, on our boat, I asked him the secret of his "magic match". He explained that he came from the Scilly Islands where in peacetime he ran a large motor boat, catering for trips around the islands.

The engine on his boat was similar to the one on the ship's boat and over the years, he had learnt this little "temporary remedy" as part of his knowledge of the engine, but he did not tell me his secret.

Finally, talent of a different nature set in a wartime atmosphere, aboard a cruiser, out in the sombre waters of Scapa Flow.

The cruiser's aircraft hangar had been transformed into a music hall for the night and as I was sleeping aboard at the time, I was able to attend and enjoy the show.

All the "artists" were members of the ship's company, while other members of the crew ensured the hangar was full of an appreciative audience.

The programme included two pianists, one who played classical music and another who played popular numbers of the day, such as "Roll out the Barrel" and "We'll meet again" during which time the whole hangar gave vocal support.

One or two stand up comedians, encouraged by their mess

mates, brought good humour and laughter to the show, while others, including a number of vocalists ensured a varied programme.

Towards the end of the evening, a tall Naval Commander, with a fine presence, and a splendid voice, stepped on to the improvised stage and sang "Rose of England".

A deep hush fell over the packed hangar, as the patriotic song in its wartime setting brought tender thoughts of loved ones at home and elsewhere. At the conclusion of the Commander's enchanting song, a prolonged and enthusiastic round of applause brought the evening's entertainment to a close.

Among the next ships I went aboard was the battleship H.M.S. Iron Duke (F.30), lying immobilised, not far from Lyness. She had been damaged earlier in the War by a bomb and in 1943 was the Headquarters of the Admiral Commanding Orkney and Shetland. Also along with other duties she provided a berth for the armed Motor

F.30 - The battleship H.M.S. Iron Duke, Admiral Jellicoe's flagship at the Battle of Jutland in 1916, during World War I (Photograph: National Maritime Museum, London)

Launches, engaged on security patrols in the Flow, and it was to work on the guns of these Motor Launches, that I travelled by boat to the "Iron Duke".

It was a wretched day, with driving rain and patches of mist making for bad visibility, as the boat edged alongside the low quarter deck of the "Iron Duke", so that I could climb aboard. As I climbed aboard I had a feeling of stepping back into history, as the "Iron Duke" had been Admiral John Jellicoe's flagship at the Battle of Jutland, in 1916, during World War I.

As I arrived on deck, clad in my oilskins, calf length boots etc. and dripping wet I must have looked a somewhat suspicious figure, for I was immediately challenged by an armed sentry with fixed bayonet and escorted below to the Security Officer.

The Security Officer checked my Scapa Flow pass, and contacted Lyness Armament Depot for confirmation, and being satisfied, detailed another naval rating to introduce me to the Motor Launches, bobbing, restlessly, alongside the "Iron Duke".

Each of the three launches I was detailed to attend to, had a 3 Pdr Hotchkiss QF gun mounted near its bow, and although the gun was introduced into the Royal Navy in 1885, it was still a very useful weapon, capable of inflicting serious damage, particularly on lightly armoured vessels.

In World War I they were used intensively by the Royal Navy and the Army, but in World War II, the Royal Navy used them mainly on Motor Launches, Auxiliary Vessels, and for saluting purposes.

By working under cover, as much as possible on component parts and avoiding the rain as much as possible, I completed the task and ensured the guns were in a serviceable condition.

Then after reporting this to the Officer of the Watch, I was ready to leave.

However, while waiting aboard the "Iron Duke" for my boat to arrive, I took shelter out of the wind and rain, below deck, and there in the region of the quarter deck, was the uniform of Admiral John Jellicoe, carefully protected in a glass case.

It was still pouring with rain, when I took my leave of the Officer of the Watch, and boarded the boat for the journey back to Lyness.

A very different commitment that came my way, started when I was detailed to service a number of guns, manned by the Royal Navy at Marwick Head, in the north of the Isle of Pomona, the largest island in the Orkney group.

I was to travel alone and any assistance I required would be supplied by the Royal Navy Detachment stationed at Marwick Head.

My instructions included the identity number of a boat that would take me across the Flow to a rendezvous on the coast of Pomona, where I was to wait by the road side for a Royal Naval Saloon car to pick me up and transport me to Marwick Head. On completion of the exercise the Officer in Charge of the Naval Unit at Marwick Head would make arrangements for my return.

In keeping with wartime instructions, I asked no questions, and early the next morning arrived at the Armament Depot to collect my tool box, before making my way down to the waterfront, where twenty or so trawlers etc. were moored alongside Lyness Quay.

After a brief search I located my boat and climbed aboard,

to be shown below into the crew's cabin, a welcome shelter from the piercing wind. Two members of the crew were my companions, as with a heavy swell running we made our way across the Flow to the shores of the Isle of Pomona.

After a considerable time travelling, one of my companions, returning from the upper deck, informed me that "this is it" and we made our way up on deck to be greeted by a grim and desolate shore line, from which there extended a derelict wooden jetty, about twenty yards long.

The jetty consisted of a series of narrow wooden planks, secured to the top of a number of wooden piles driven into the seabed. The jetty had obviously never possessed handrails and in the distant past, had probably served a temporary purpose of some kind.

Owing to the heavy swell, the skipper shouted down from his steering cabin, that he dare not go alongside the jetty for fear of smashing it to pieces. He would, however, put the bow of the boat as near as possible to the jetty and I could either jump or step off the boat, which ever proved the most opportune.

Everything went to plan, I made it with a short jump, and my precious tool box was slid across the bow of the boat, for me to grasp its handle and pull it up to safety.

The boat immediately backed off from the jetty, leaving me crouched low, against a strong wind, as holding my tool box in one hand, as an anchor, I made my way up the gently swaying jetty to heave a sigh of relief, as I reached the shore.

A short distance from the jetty was a small dilapidated, wooden hut with an open front that faced onto a narrow, deserted road, set in a deserted landscape. This apparently was my rendezvous with the naval saloon car.

I quickly took what shelter the hut had to offer from the biting wind and spent the next half an hour, popping in and out of the hut, making sure that the driver of the car, did not flash by and report back "that there was no-one at the rendezvous".

Eventually a Royal Navy saloon car drove into sight, and with a shriek of brakes, pulled up near the hut.

Then, after identifying myself to the Wren driver and confirming my destination with her, I settled down in the car as we sped along deserted roads on our way north.

Arriving at the Marwick Head Royal Naval station, I reported to the Officer in Charge who explained to me that it was a bank of four 2 Pdr Mk VIII QF guns that required attention.

So, after being shown to my living accommodation and meeting the two naval ratings who would assist me in the morning, I took a preliminary look at the guns.

One gun was leaking water from the muzzle gland that retained the cooling water that surrounded the barrel. This would probably need a new gland packing if the gland nut had already been fully tightened.

As regards the Royal Naval Station, it had the appearance of a frontier outpost, with its group of buildings, dominated by a Royal Navy ensign flying above them.

During the next four days, ably assisted by the two naval ratings, I stripped each of the guns, which were mounted to fire seaward removing for examination, each gun's automatic mechanism, the large spiral recoil spring that surrounded the barrel, and the barrel itself, that weighed 112 lbs (approx. 51 kgs).

One of the ratings obtained a new muzzle gland packing, from the station's stock of gun spares and this stopped the leak. Finally, after all the guns had been reassembled, their water jackets were refilled, with water, their buffer systems "topped up" with a mixture of glycerine and water, and their firing mechanisms checked, to bring the work to a successful conclusion.

Then having reported to the Officer in Charge that his guns were fully serviceable and ready for use, I decided to have a look at the area outside the Royal Naval Station, where a steep gully, with a few cottages lining its slopes, ran out to meet the sea.

I spoke to several of the people living in the cottages, who, recalled events relating to the sinking of the cruiser H.M.S. Hampshire, by a mine, off Marwick Head, on the 5th June 1916 during World War I.

They spoke of how the nearby coasts, including the gully were searched for survivors.

Also, nearby on Marwick Head, there is a Memorial Tower, erected to commemorate the disaster in which Field Marshal Earl Kitchener and many others lost their lives.

The Monument bears the following inscription. "This Tower was erected by the people of Orkney, in memory of Field Marshal Earl Kitchener of Khartoum, on that corner of his country, which he had served so faithfully, nearest to the place where he died on duty.

He and his staff perished, along with the officers and nearly all the men of H.M.S. Hampshire on the 5th June 1916".

I made my way back to the Naval Station to prepare for my departure in the morning.

Then it all happened, a terrific storm hit the Headland, with howling winds and torrential rain, putting restrictions on most land and water transport.

It forestalled any plans I had of leaving, and raged for two days and nights, during which time I enjoyed the hospitality of the Royal Navy.

The night before I left, the Officer in Charge asked me to take a gun back to Lyness. To this I readily agreed, and at the same time conjured up a mental picture of a revolver, a rifle, or at the most a light machine gun.

However, came the dawn, the weather had cleared, and having thanked the Officer in Charge for the hospitality I had received and said cheerio to the members of the mess, I received possession of the gun.

It was a 12 Pdr QF gun barrel only weighing 11.5 cwt (approx. 585 kgs) and accompanied by a Naval Party, equipped with lifting ropes and hand spikes, all assembled ready to assist me.

We loaded the gun barrel onto a lorry then we all climbed aboard and headed for a landing venue, with a solid concrete quay, as opposed to the rickety jetty of my earlier acquaintance.

The Naval Party made short work of putting the gun aboard the waiting fishing boat and safely securing it with ropes.

Then, off they went, in their lorry, back to their duties at Marwick Head, while I settled down aboard the boat for the trip back to Lyness. On arrival at Lyness, I made arrangements for the gun barrel to be "picked up" and retired to reflect on another interesting spell of duty.

I experienced feelings of gratitude and satisfaction from the gun work I performed at Marwick Head. Where, for over a period of six days and nights, and while working in a remote area, I had received the Royal Navy's traditional welcome and hospitality from the members of a small Royal Navy unit stationed at Marwick Head.

Towards the end of 1943 a regular army unit of the Gordon Highlanders, who were encamped in the Lyness area, received their orders to leave Orkney and as a tribute to them, the Lyness detachment of the Seaforth Highlanders Home Guard gave "a Farewell to the Gordons" party in their honour.

Lyness provided the venue, for what proved to be a rather boisterous evening, with the "Seaforths" acting as stewards, bar tenders etc. to ensure that everyone enjoyed themselves.

Another Home Guard and I ran the cloakroom, a task that limited our movements but we took it in turn to have a look at the colourful and most energetic proceedings taking place on the dance floor.

The order of the day for the "Gordons" was full regimental dress, with kilts and trews very much in evidence. A group of splendidly attired pipers provided stirring music as a variety of Scottish dances and reels were performed.

As the evening wore on the dancing got more robust and vigorous, and at one stage the dance floor was cleared to allow a series of traditional highland Sword dances to be performed.

Our "Farewell to the Gordons" went on into the early hours of the morning, and finished up with much handshaking and backslapping, as they departed, taking with them our very best wishes for whatever lay ahead of them.

As December 1943 drew to a close, I spent a week or so including Christmas Day and Boxing Day victualled aboard the 31,100 ton (approx. 31, 606 tonnes), battleship H.M.S. Valiant (F.31) which took part in World War I and was attached to the 5th Battle Squadron at the Battle of Jutland in 1916.

The great battleship with her minimum complement of 1,000 men, had a powerful armament of eight 15" BL guns, and many anti-aircraft guns, including several mountings of four 2 Pdr MK VIII QF guns, on which I was employed.

My work on the 2 Pdr mountings had gone very well despite the bitter wind and heavy flurries of snow that had interrupted progress on several occasions.

F.31 - H.M.S. Valiant, a 31,100 ton battleship on which I spent Christmas 1943 (Photo: Royal Naval Museum, HMS Naval Base, Portsmouth)

F.32 - A New Year Card for 1944, purchased while I was working aboard a destroyer out in the Flow

There was also one very pleasing morning when after I had stripped one of the 2 Pdr guns and laid out its component parts for my own examination, that I observed a senior officer making his way along the deserted deck towards me.

He was well muffled up against the weather, and was wearing a short, thick, navy blue top coat, with a neatly arranged navy blue scarf around his neck, while his every movement as he approached the gun mounting, exuded an air of authority.

When he reached the gun mounting, we passed the time of day and he enquired how the work on the guns was going, in response to which I gave him a precise account of progress to date.

Then, in a casual manner, he asked me what the Snib Gib was on a 2 Pdr Mk VIII gun. Never in my life have I been so pleased that I knew what a Snib Gib was and could answer his question.

It was, in fact, one of the smallest and most obscure parts of the gun, being a spring loaded plunger, about 1" long and ½" wide, and was part of the cartridge extractor.

By using the cartridge extractor from the gun that I had stripped I was able to show him a Snib Gib and explain its function in assisting to keep the cartridge in its correct position in the extractor.

He seemed well pleased with our conversation and with the glimmer of a smile on his face, added "I heard something about a Snib Gib, when on a gunnery course some years ago", and then with a nod of approval he passed sedately on his way.

I have often reflected since then, if he was the Officer in Command of H.M.S. Valiant.

The gun work progressed with no undue problems, and come Christmas Day I was still aboard the "Valiant" sharing messing arrangements with several Dockyard men.

In the true Christmas spirit, one of the ship's cooks made us a Christmas cake and we returned the compliment by having a "whip round" and presenting him with the financial proceeds.

So, aided by our tots of rum, we celebrated Christmas 1943 aboard H.M.S. Valiant.

We were still aboard on Boxing Day, when the news came through that a Naval battle had taken place off the North Cape of Norway, in which the German battleship Scharnhorst had been sunk, while endeavouring to attack a British convoy bound for Russia.

Later reports, from elsewhere, included the following information.

At around 9.30am on Boxing Day, 26th December 1943, the German battleship Scharnhorst, operating off the North Cape of Norway, located a British convoy bound for Russia. In the dim light of the Artic Winter, she closed on the convoy intent on destroying it with her nine 11" and twelve 5.9" guns.

Powerful units of the Royal Navy, including the 14" gun battleship H.M.S. Duke of York, the cruisers H.M.S. Belfast, Norfolk, Sheffield and Jamaica, supported by destroyers, engaged the Scharnhorst and after making two attempts to attack the convoy the Scharnhorst endeavoured to escape.

At this stage, a 14" shell from the "Duke of York" hit the Scharnhorst and greatly reduced her speed. In this condition, the Scharnhorst was hit again and again by devastating shell fire, and also suffered severe damage from torpedo attacks launched by the destroyers and cruisers and at 7.45pm on Boxing Day 26th December 1943, the Scharnhorst was sunk.

Shortly after this Naval action and while crossing the Flow in the Department's boat I was privileged to witness a most spectacular and moving sight, for bearing down on our boat, were the ships returning from the battle of North Cape.

They were being led in by the Norwegian destroyer, "Stord" as a tribute to the Norwegian Nation, and the part she herself had played in the action.

We moved clear, and with our engines ticking over at dead slow, I had a splendid view of the historical scene as the ships sailed up the Flow with the "Duke of York" towering above them like some gigantic floating fortress.

The crews of the ships in the Flow "lined ship" in the traditional Royal Navy fashion to cheer the ships as they sailed by.

The cheering took the form of a "wave of sound" as successive ships in the line took up the cheering. While each ship took on a pronounced list under the weight of members of the crew as they lined one side only of the ship.

Thus the ships returning from the Battle of North Cape passed up the Flow, and into Naval history, as they took up their appointed anchorages.

By this time, my sights were set on the 15th January 1944, when officially my six months spell of duty in Orkney was due to come to an end, and all being well I would be returned to my home base at Chatham.

In the meantime, I returned my Seaforth Highlanders uniform, had a last physical culture session in my allotted space in the local cinema and said cheerio to the staff at the Lyness Armament Depot.

The day of my departure duly arrived and with my pass allowing me to return to the Scottish mainland I passed through the security office aboard the "Dunluce Castle" to board a boat for Thurso.

It was a fairly calm crossing of the Pentland Forth, with only a slight swell running. On arriving at Thurso, there was a short wait for a train, on which there were plenty of seats and I made myself comfortable as the train headed south for London.

Arriving in London early next morning and with no train to Chatham at that hour, I took a stroll outside the deserted station, to find a huge fire burning in a nearby block of buildings, with fireman silhouetted against the skyline as they fought to bring the blazing inferno under control. Apparently there had been a German raid not long before.

There was a Lyons "all night" restaurant near the station and I went in for several cups of coffee, sharing a table, in the crowded restaurant, with four uniformed members of the Royal Canadian Artillery, who were busily engaged in consuming the contents of their hip flasks. I gently declined their invitation to join them in their drinking and made my way back to the station, where I spent the rest of the night, trying in vain to sleep on a platform seat.

Early the next morning I caught the first train from London to Chatham, arriving at our house at about 6.30 am, where in answer to my knocking, my wife Joyce opened the door, and welcomed me home.

CHAPTER 8

Armament Work in H.M. Dockyard, Chatham

January 1944 to Victory in Europe (VE) Day

8th May 1945

On returning home from the Orkneys, I reported back to H.M. Gunwharf Chatham and then rejoined the Afloat Party in Chatham Dockyard.

I also received an offer of a transfer from the Chatham Town Unit of the Royal West Kent Regiment Home Guard to "D" Company 31st (Chatham Dockyard) Battalion of the Royal West Kent Regiment Home Guard, as an Instructor on Close Combat, Assault and Obstacle Courses. An offer which I readily accepted.

On the 5th May 1944, I obtained my Certificate "A" (F.33) which allowed me to conduct courses on these subjects without supervision and I was promoted to Lance Corporal.

I took up my duties at the Royal Engineers' Gymnasium at Old Brompton, near Gillingham, Kent, and it was really something to have the use of this large gymnasium and I put in many extra training sessions on my own, as well as conducting the Courses.

The Obstacle Course was sited not far from the Gymnasium, and two of its obstacles were a moat and a construction of girders. The moat, which surrounded some old fortifications, had to be crossed by means of ropes stretched across its width. The girder construction was required to be climbed and then traversed along its length.

F.33 - A Home Guard Instructors' Certificate in 1944

Many of the Home Guardsmen were very fit - there were some tough jobs in the Dockyard - and they took the obstacles in a very efficient manner.

On one occasion, the Regular Army and the Home Guard staff at the Royal Engineers' Gymnasium arranged an interesting exhibition of Judo, given by regular Army Instructors. In the region of 200 Regular Army and Home Guard personnel attended.

A full size boxing ring, erected in the Gymnasium provided the platform for the exhibition, and five or six Instructors, clad in the traditional, strongly made, white jackets and trousers, secured in all cases by black belts, signifying the instructors top level in Judo qualifications, gave a rather frightening performance of Judo throws and holds, as bodies hit the deck in all directions.

Following this, an announcement from the ring invited members of the audience to step up and enjoy the virtues of a "stomach throw" a "flying mare" or a "strangle hold".

A strong silence fell over the audience, due no doubt to the too recent memory of bodies hitting the deck.

Then followed a very humorous episode that added much to the evening's entertainment. An Officer sitting near the front row, stood up to his full six foot, and very slowly and methodically removed his top coat, and neatly folding it up, placed it on the empty seat beside him. This brought a ripple of admiration from the audience, as they prepared to see him enter the ring.

However, the Officer equally slowly and methodically resumed his seat, causing a voice from the ring to enquire "Are you coming up Sir?" to which the Officer replied in a cultured voice "Good God no, I just felt a bit hot that's all". Everybody enjoyed the episode including the black belted Instructors, who had already begun to flex their muscles.

In the Dockyard, "Hunt" Class destroyers occupied some of my time, with their main armament of four, twin mounted 4" Mk XVI QF guns.

The "Hunt" Class destroyers commenced being built in 1939, and in the region of sixty of them were built. They were named after hunting packs and included such names as "Southdown", "Cotswold", "Hambledon" and "Quantock", and while employed on these vessels, I often heard the "attention call" of "Tally Ho! Tally Ho!" coming over the ship's loudspeakers.

Another gun trial on a destroyer came my way, and took place off the coast of Kent, and after successful gun trials had been completed, the destroyer proceeded up the east coast of England in order to carry out night exercises in other aspects of the ship.

The exercise that I witnessed from a safe vantage point was

a dangerous one, and took place in total darkness with the destroyer travelling at speed.

It commenced with one of the ship's life boats being lifted high in its davits and its crew in life jackets climbing aboard.

Next the boat was swung outboard and lowered over the side, until it hung suspended a safe distance above the water as the destroyer continued to travel at speed.

After remaining suspended for ten minutes or so, the boat was brought back inboard and the crew climbed out. The lifeboat was then made secure and the exercise came to an end.

During 1944, Kent and the South Coast area were still the scene of aerial activity and on Tuesday 13th June 1944, what appeared to be a damaged German aircraft, with flames shooting out from its tail section, flew over Kent in the direction of London, and fell on waste land at Swanscombe in Kent.

It was, in fact, one of Germany's secret weapons, known as the V1 flying bomb, which the British public, with their well known sense of humour, quickly named the "Doodle Bug".

The V1s were pilot-less and had the appearance of a low winged mono-plane. They were loaded with explosives and the flames from the tail came from the propulsion unit.

The propulsion unit was preset to "cut out" when over the target area in this case London, causing the V1 to plunge to earth and explode with devastating effect. They were launched from sites in German occupied territories across the Channel.

Strangely enough, and also very unexpectedly, I had a very close view of the underside of a V1 when on a visit to the Open Air Swimming Pool, at Gillingham in Kent, near to Chatham Dockyard.

The pool was virtually deserted as I lay in the water, floating almost motionless on my back, when a V1 suddenly appeared and flew rather low, straight over the swimming pool.

I continued to lay on top of the water, gazing upwards at the V1, during which time I virtually felt no reaction to its presence, except a rather belated feeling of disbelief and relief as it sped on its way and no immediate explosion followed.

A report dated 15th September 1944, and published as a supplement in the "Kent Messenger" newspaper, stated that 8,000 V1s were launched, of which 1,388 were shot down or came down on Kentish soil, while a further 1,000 were shot down into the sea from the Kent coast and 2,200 fell on London. Sussex and neighbouring areas also suffered from V1 attacks and successfully destroyed many V1s.

My last major gun fitting job of World War II, was on one of the mighty 15" BL guns stored on the Gun Ground in Chatham Dockyard.

The following details and F.34 and F.35 give a little idea of the size of the gun:-

Weight of Gun - 97 tons 3 cwt (approx. 98.73 tonnes).

Weight of Breech Mechanism - 2 tons 17 cwt (approx. 2.9 tonnes).

Overall length of Gun - 650.4 ins (approx 16.7m).

Weight of Shells - 17 cwt 34 lbs / 17 cwt 16 lbs.

Maximum range at 30° elevation - 33,550 yards (approx. 30,676 m) (approx 19.06 miles).

The requirement was to fit and assemble the breech mechanism and its supplementary equipment to the gun (F.34 and F.35), while additional work involved drilling and hand tapping, to form threads in the barrel of the gun, for the purpose of screwing airblast and electrical components to the gun.

A drawing of the drilling equipment, dating back to 1864,

that I used to drill the holes on the circumference of the gun in aid of the air blast equipment, is shown in F.36. It gave excellent service and enabled drilling to be carried out on the gun in a difficult position.

I was given two very experienced "fitter's mates" to assist me and the component parts of the breech mechanism having arrived, the job got under way.

F.34 - A 15" Gun and its shells on display in the forecourt of the Imperial War Museum, London

For lifting purposes, the 100 ton Gantry Crane that straddled the Gun Ground was moved so that its massive steel hook was positioned above the breech end of the gun.

A manually operated "chain lifting block" was then suspended from the hook of the crane and only the "chain lifting block" was used for lifting and by this method, coupled with a slight movement of the Gantry Crane as required, the lifting and positioning of the heavy components could be controlled within inches. The Gantry Crane alone did not readily bend itself to such flexibility. Much of the work was also carried out from a wooden platform specially erected around the breech end of the gun.

F.35 - The Breech Mechanism of a 15" Gun

The whole job proved to be a very exacting and physically demanding one, as I always thought it would be, but with splendid assistance from my two "fitter's mates" the breech mechanism gradually took shape and the additional work was also completed and it was nearly time for an Examiner of Naval Ordnance to "pass out" the gun.

A successful "pass out" duly followed and the giant gun was ready for issue.

To the best of my knowledge, this was the only 15" BL gun worked on in this manner, in Chatham Dockyard during

World War II. I was also left with the firm conviction that physically, it was a young man's job, and being around 32 years of age at the time, I guess I came into that category.

From then onwards, until the end of World War II, I continued to work with my good humoured companions of the Afloat Party in Chatham Dockyard, with occasional visits to Sheerness Dockyard.

Following the "D" Day Landings in France on 6th June 1944, Paris was liberated, and on the 4th May 1945, the German Armed Forces in Holland, Denmark and Northern Germany surrendered to Field Marshal Montgomery.

The 8th May 1945 was designated "Victory in Europe", VE Day, and thanksgiving services and celebrations for peace took place throughout Great Britain, and other countries.

In the evening, my wife Joyce and I, with our three year old son Richard in his push chair, made our way to Chatham Town Hall, where hundreds of people with feelings of joy, relief and sorrow had gathered to celebrate and give thanks for peace.

The celebrations went on late into the night, but before the crowd began to break up, my wife, son and I wended our way home to bring this true story of World War II to a happy ending.

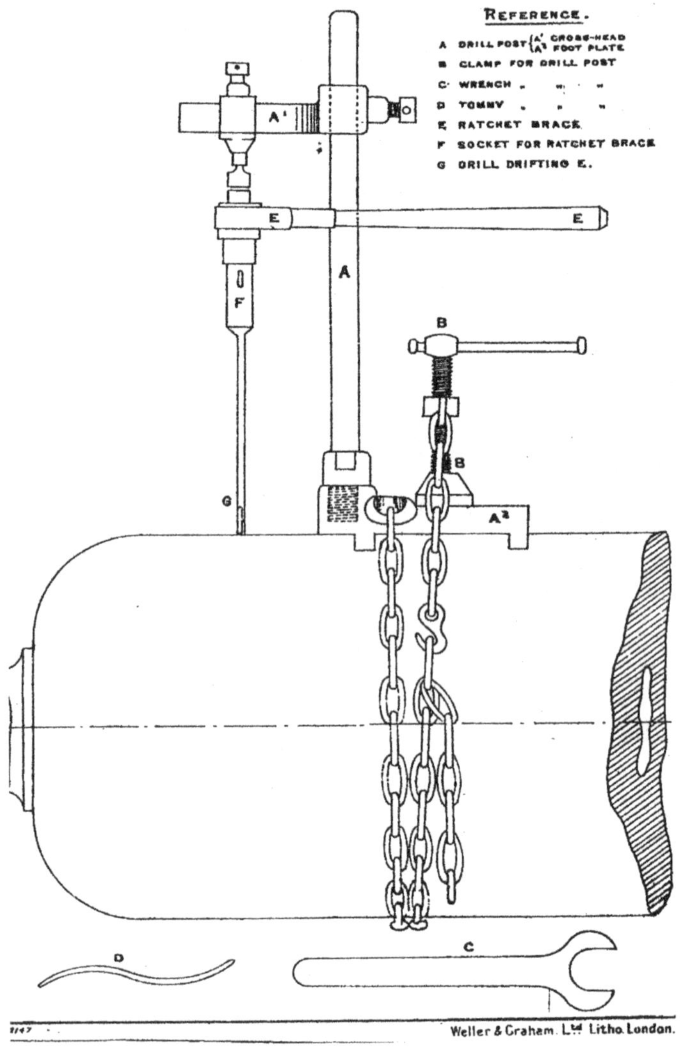

F.36 - The equipment used for drilling holes in the circumference of the 15" Gun on the Gun Ground in H.M. Dockyard, Chatham

APPENDIX 1

Programme of the visit of His Majesty King George VI, to the Home Fleet at Scapa Flow, Orkney, from 12th to 15th August 1943

From the Royal Archives, by kind permission of the Royal Collection Trust

His Majesty the King intends to visit the Home Fleet at Scapa Flow from Thursday 12th August to Sunday 15th August 1943. His Majesty will stay with the Commander in Chief in His Majesty's Ship, DUKE OF YORK during the visit.

Thursday 12th August

1. His Majesty will arrive at Thurso by train at 1400 on Thursday 12th August and will embark at Scrabster in a destroyer for the passage to Scapa escorted by destroyers. The Vice Admiral Commanding Orkney and Shetland will meet His Majesty at Thurso and will accompany him on board the destroyer.

2. On arrival in the Flow, at about 1600, His Majesty will transfer to H.M.S. Duke of York and will be received on board by the Commander in Chief Home Fleet. The Flag Officers of the Home Fleet will be presented to His Majesty on his arrival on board H.M.S. Duke of York. The Royal Standard will be broken in the DUKE OF

YORK when His Majesty first arrives on board. It will be transferred to PHOEBE on His Majesty's departure. After tea His Majesty will visit H.M. Australian S. SHROPSHIRE and will then visit H.M.S. TYNE. Detachments from Home Fleet destroyers will be assembled on board the TYNE.

There will be a dinner party on board H.M.S. DUKE OF YORK.

Friday 13th August

3. His Majesty will inspect the Ships' Companies of certain ships during the forenoon. Ships which cannot be visited will individually send detachments to the ships visited.

4. His Majesty will watch the firing of the Scapa barrage at 12.15 from the ANSON and will lunch on board the ANSON.

5. After lunch His Majesty will visit His Hellenic Majesty's Ship THEMISTOCLES berthed alongside H.M.S. ANSON and will then land at Sutherland Pier.

6. His Majesty will attend the Fleet Concert at the Flotta Theatre during the afternoon and will have tea at the Officers' Club, Flotta.

7. His Majesty will visit H.M. India Sloop GODAVARI on his way back to the DUKE OF YORK and he will visit the submarine berthed alongside the DUKE OF YORK on return.

8. There will be a dinner party in the DUKE OF YORK.

Saturday 14th August

9.   His Majesty will go to sea in the DUKE OF YORK for exercises. Ships taking part will get underway about 0945 returning to harbour by 1800.

His Majesty will lunch in the Wardroom of the DUKE OF YORK and will have tea in the Gunroom.

10.   There will be no formal function arranged for Saturday evening.

Sunday 15th August

11.   His Majesty will visit H.M.S. Belfast after which he will attend a special service ashore in the Flotta Theatre. Representatives from as many outlying units in the Orkney Command as possible will be at this service.

12.   After the service His Majesty will meet, informally, welfare workers on Flotta who will be assembled in the Church of Scotland hut.

He will then return to the DUKE OF YORK.

13.   His Majesty will leave the DUKE OF YORK at 11.45 and will embark in H.M.S. PHOEBE for passage to Scrabster. He will have lunch on board H.M.S. PHOEBE.

14.   His Majesty will land at Scrabster about 1330 and will leave Thurso by train at 1400.

BRUCE FRASER

ADMIRAL

Together with further instructions and information related to the visit, the programme was distributed as follows:-

Distribution:-

The Naval Secretary to the First Lord of the Admiralty (and for Sir Eric Mierville K.C.I.E).

Vice Admiral Commanding Orkney and Shetland.

Vice Admiral Second in Command Home Fleet.

Rear Admiral Commanding Tenth Cruiser Squadron.

Rear Admiral (D) (and for destroyers "Themistocles" and "Godavari").

Admiral Superintendent Orkney

Commanding Officers H.M. Ships, Duke of York, Anson, Renown, Malay, London, Danoe, Tyne, Belfast, Ceylon, Phoebe, H.M.A.S. Shropshire.

APPENDIX 2

H.M. Gunwharf Chatham

1666 to 1958

Reference:- Naval Armament Journal No 15 April 1959

The Gunwharf site was first used for Naval Service in 1547, when a storehouse in the vicinity of St Mary's Church, Chatham was rented. Additional storehouses were rented during 1548 to 1550, when an Order in Council instructed that "all the Kings ships should be harboured in Gillingham Water" (that part of the R Medway near to the Gunwharf), save those that be at Portsmouth. The site was known as Gillingham Dockyard.

During the reign of Queen Elizabeth I (1558 to 1603), the Dockyard expanded further down the river and in 1567 the Dockyard was renamed Chatham Dockyard, and in 1666 the original site, near to St Mary's Church, Chatham was transferred by the Admiralty to the Board of Ordnance, headed by the Master General of Ordnance.

From 1666, until it closed on 30th December 1958 the Gunwharf was controlled by the following Government Departments, during which time Naval and Army guns and other armament stores were stored and repaired there.

DEPARTMENT	**PERIOD**
Board of Ordnance	1666 to May 1855
Caretakers Control by Government Officials	1855 to 1856
War Department	1857 to 1891
Admiralty	1st October 1891 to 30th December 1958

APPENDIX 3

HM Dockyard Chatham

1567 to 1984

Information kindly supplied by
The Chatham Historical Dockyard Society, including
A Short History of Chatham Dockyard by David Hunter
(Chatham Navy Days Magazine 1982)

As related in Appendix 2, which deals with H.M. Gunwharf, Chatham, Chatham Dockyard received its title in 1562, having previously been known as Gillingham Dockyard.

Chatham Dockyard served the Royal Navy from 1567 to 1984, a period of 417 years. In 1984 however, as a result of extensive changes in Government naval policies, Chatham Dockyard closed down.

Three items from the Dockyard's vast catalogue of events are as follows;-

1720 - The building of the Dockyard's elegant Main Gate (F.13) was completed.

1759 to 1765 - During this time, H.M.S. Victory, a first rate of 100 guns, was built and launched in 1765. This was Admiral Nelson's flagship at the Battle of Trafalgar in 1805.

1844 - Around this time, Chatham Dockyard School
for Dockyard Apprentices was established.

During World War II, 1939 to 1945, the maximum number
employed in the Dockyard was 13,000 of whom 2,000 were
women. Many reservists, territorials and other employees were
called up for War Service.

A total of 1,360 ships were taken in hand during World War
II, for repair, refit, modernisation or conversions. This
involved 804 dry dockings.

In addition to this, 10 submarines, a cruiser, 2 mooring
vessels, 2 sloops and a floating dock were built and 64 vessels
were fitted out for special service, while 31 vessels built in
Chatham Dockyard served in World War II.

The Dockyard Telephone Exchange was transferred to an
underground shelter, and gun towers and emplacements were
constructed and connected to the gun operations room. The
number of air raid alerts was 1,369 and 92 high explosive
bombs were dropped on the Dockyard, together with
numerous incendiary bombs and 15 persons were killed and
107 injured.

APPENDIX 4

**H.M. Dockyard Sheerness 1665 to 1958
and Queenborough Minesweeping Base 1939 to 1945**

References:- Information on H.M. Dockyard Sheerness, kindly supplied by Sheerness Library, Sheerness, Kent and the pamphlet "H.M.S. Wildfire and Queenborough Minesweeping Base 1939 to 1945", prepared with assistance from many contributors by Swale Borough and Queenborough Town Councils

Sheerness Dockyard was situated on the right bank of the R Medway, near to its estuary, and initial work on its construction took place during the period 1665 to 1667, while major work on extending its workshops and other facilities, including dry docks was commenced in 1825, under the direction of the architect Mr Rennie.

The Dockyard dealt, in the main, with the smaller type of naval craft, such as destroyers, submarines and trawlers. Also adjoining the Dockyard, and closely associated with it, was H.M.S. Wildfire, the Royal Naval shore establishment and barracks which was built in 1889.

Following the end of World War I, 1914 to 1918, the workforce in the Dockyard was greatly reduced, and it was not until the 1930's that work in the Dockyard increased and a growing number of shipwrights were recruited.

During World War II, 1939 to 1945, the experienced staff of the Dockyard performed an important role in maintaining and repairing ships of the Fleet.

In May 1940 the Dockyard's Middle Camber was used as the assembly centre for a large number of the ships that took part in the Evacuation of the British Expeditionary Force from Dunkirk. The ships assembled in the Middle Camber included 100 motor boats, 10 lighters, 7 Dutch skoots and 6 Paddle Steamers.

During the Evacuation of Dunkirk, a total of 338,226 members of the British Expeditionary Force, who were in danger of being overrun by the overwhelming German onslaught were brought back safely to Britain. At the same time members of the French forces were also evacuated safely back to Britain.

Following the end of World War II, the Dockyard continued to serve the Royal Navy but changes in Government polices brought about the closure of a number of major Admiralty establishments, including Sheerness Dockyard, and on Tuesday 19th February 1958 it was announced in the House of Lords that Sheerness Dockyard would close.

So after a period of around 293 years service to the Royal Navy, Sheerness Dockyard closed, with the loss of 3,000 jobs.

About 2 miles upstream from Sheerness was the port of Queenborough on the Isle of Sheppey and here in 1939 the Queenborough Minesweeping Base was established and named "Wildfire 2".

In July 1941, however, it was renamed as St Tudno, after the Liverpool passenger ship St Tudno, which had become the depot ship for the base.

The minesweepers at this stage were mostly trawlers, drifters and other fishing craft converted for the purpose, but as the War went on purpose built ships joined the minesweeping flotillas. It was an extremely dangerous task for the crews of the minesweepers as they swept the estuaries of the R Thames and R Medway as well as sweeping as far south as Ramsgate and as far north as East Anglia and at the height of the War, Captain M/S Sheerness, Captain H Hopper RN, had over 100 vessels under his command, operating out of the Queenborough Base.

APPENDIX 5

Breech Loading and Quick Firing Guns

In the case of Breech Loading guns the shell was loaded and rammed home into the gun, followed by the cordite propellant charge, or charges, contained in cloth bags which were loaded into the chamber of the gun to the rear of the shell. The breech was then closed ready for firing.

On firing, the cordite in the gun chamber was ignited by means of a firing tube inserted into the firing lock of the breech mechanism where it was detonated. The flame from the firing tube passed through a vent into the chamber and ignited the cordite charge.

The propellant gases were prevented from escaping to the rear of the gun by means of a sealing system involving an "obturating pad", made of either asbestos or neoprene. When the gun was fired the pad was compressed against a precisely machined and carefully maintained "cone shaped seating" at the entrance to the chamber and sealed the chamber.

Quick firing guns used brass cartridge case ammunition to contain the cordite propellant charge, which was ignited by means of a detonator screwed into the base of the cartridge case and the resulting explosion caused the tapered cartridge case to expand against the similarly tapered sides of the chamber and prevent the propellant gases escaping to the rear.

In addition to containing the cordite charge, the cartridge case also had the shell securely crimped into the nose of the case. This arrangement was known as "fixed ammunition" and enabled the two to be loaded together, which enhanced the rate of fire. "Separate Ammunition" in which the cartridge case and the shell were loaded separately was also used in certain calibres of QF guns.

The shells used by Breech Loading and Quick Firing guns had a copper "driving band" encircling them, near to the base of the shell. It protruded slightly above the surface of the shell, and when the gun was fired, the "driving band" "bit" into the spiral rifling of the gun and as the shell travelled up the bore of the gun the spiral rifling imparted a twisting motion to the shell, about its longitudinal axis, that increased the shell's range and improved its accuracy.

APPENDIX 6

**Broken Firing Pins in 3 Pdr Hotchkiss
QF Saluting Guns
List of Change No 6285 – 22nd August 1890
Hook Drill, Steel 6pr and 3pr**

A pattern and drawing have been sealed of the above mentioned article to govern supply.

It is intended for use with the Hotchkiss 6pr and 3pr guns at drill, to prevent the breaking of the firing pin by "snapping" the gun.

It is of steel and the loop is intended to receive the lower branch of the main spring, when unhooked from the stirrup, the upper end being passed over the projecting arms of the stirrup, previously occupied by the spring.

The arrangement admits of the spring being somewhat extended and therefore not so powerful in action.

Authors note – As the "Steel Hook" is used for drill purposes only, it may still be necessary, on other occasions, to ease the striker forward by means of the gun's re-cocking lever.

APPENDIX 7

The Holman Projector

Part of the List of Successful Engagements with Enemy Aircraft in World War II, when Holman Projectors were used. Details by kind permission of the Holman Museum, Camborne, Cornwall.

H.M. Ships

Date	Ship	Success Credited	Weapons Used
26.1.1941	H.M.S. Reids	1 confirmed	Holman & Lewis M/C Gun
26.1.1941	H.M.S. Lord St Vincent	1 confirmed	Holman & Lewis M/C Gun
12.2.1941	H.M.S. Eager	1 confirmed	Holman & Lewis M/C Gun
27.2.1941	H.M.S. Lord Stonehaven	1 damaged	0.5 " Vickers M/C Gun, Lewis M/C Gun & Holman
2.4.1941	H.M.S. Silver Dawn	1 damaged	2 Pdr Lewis M/C & Holman
9.4.1941	H.M.S. Avondale & Lord Nuffield	1 confirmed	Hotchkiss M/C Gun, 12 Pdr QF Gun, Lewis, M/C Gun Holman
27.4.1941	H.M.S. Patia	1 confirmed & Holman	3" QF Gun, 2 Pdr, Hotchkiss M/C Gun
18.5.1941	H.M.S. Corinthian	1 damaged	Hotchkiss M/C Gun, 12 Pdr QF Gun & Holman

Date	Ship	Success Credited	Weapons Used
28.7.1941	H.M.S. Typhoon	1 confirmed	12 Pdr QF Gun, Hotchkiss M/C Gun, Lewis M/C Gun & Holman
4.8.1941	H.M.S. Norland	1 confirmed	12 Pdr QF Gun, Lewis M/C Gun & Holman
15.7.1942`	H.M.L. 141 & 1 damaged	1 confirmed	0.5" Vickers M/C Gun, Lewis M/C Gun & Holman
15.7.1942	H.M.L.139	1 probable	0.5" Vickers M/C Gun, Lewis M/C Gun & Holman

Merchant Ships

Date	Ship	Success Credited	Weapons Used
1.6.1940	S/S Bombay	1 probable	Holman
1.8.1940	S/S Highlander	1 confirmed	Holman & Lewis M/C Gun
8.12.1940	S/S Treverbyn	1 damaged	Hotchkiss M/C Gun & Holman
20.2.1941	M.V.D.L Harper	1 damaged	Hotchkiss M/C Gun & Holman
13.3.1941	S/S Inishtrahull	1 damaged	Holman & Machine Guns
23.3.1941	S/S Beltoy	1 probable	12 Pdr QF Gun, Lewis M/C Gun & Holman
6.4.1941	M/V Adoni	1 damaged	Hotchkiss M/C Gun, Lewis M/C Gun & Holman
18.4.1941	F/T Kingsway & Tracian	1 confirmed	Lewis M/C Gun & Holman
27.4.1941	S/S Marie Dawn	1 confirmed	Hotchkiss M/C Gun Lewis M/C Gun & Holman
4.5.1941	M/V Araybank	2 confirmed	Hotchkiss M/C Gun & Holman
20.6.1941	S/S Dalemoor & Others	1 probable	Hotchkiss M/C Gun, Lewis M/C Gun & Holman
20.6.1941	S/S Lanark	1 damaged	Hotchkiss M/C Gun, Lewis M/C Gun, P.A.C. & Holman

APPENDIX 8

**HM Ships mentioned in the book and in
most cases worked on.**

The numbers donate the related Chapters.

H.M Ships:- Anson 7   Arethusa 3   Belfast 7   Crested Eagle 1   Reserve Fleet Destroyers:- 1   Duke of York 7 Euryalus 1   Exeter:- 1   H.M New Zealand Ship   Gambia 7 Hostile 3 "Hunt" Class Destroyers:- 8   Iron Duke 7 Ivanhoe 3   Jamaica 7   Keith 3   Kenya 5   Malacolite 4 Malaya 7   Marshall Soulti 1   Medway Queen 1   Motor Launches 7 Nelson 7 Norfolk 7   Pelican 3   Queen of Kent 1   Queen of Thanet 1   Renown 7   Rolls Royce 4 Rose Hilda 2   Royal Daffodil 1   Royal Eagle 1   Royal Marine 4   Royal Sovereign 1   Salmon 3   Sheffield 7 Southampton 6   H.M Australian Ship Shropshire 7 "Tribal" Class Destroyers 3   United States Destroyer transferred to the Royal Navy 3   Valiant 7   "V" and "IV" Class Destroyer 1   Worcester 1   York 1

Allied Naval Ships mentioned:-   Norwegian Navy Ship "Stord" 7   Polish Navy Ship "Dragon" 6   Assistance to a United States Navy Ship 3

Made in the USA
Monee, IL
07 July 2026

56552035R00095